To TERRY

NICE TO MEET
AND
ENTERTAIN YOU!

13-7-2020

1

SOUTHERN ROOTS – Part 1

A Rock'n'Roll Story 1958 -1972

By

David St John

First published by DSJP

Other titles by the same author:

YOURS QUIZZICALLY – CONFESSIONS OF A TV QUIZ ADDICT

THE LIFE OF 'KIWI' BRIAN

THE SOUTHERN ENTERTAINER

Available via Amazon Books

COPYRIGHT

Front cover photograph - the author 1958

CHAPTERS:

DEDICATION

This book is dedicated to the memory of my uncle Arthur Marshall, who was suddenly taken away by the outbreak of the global Corona Virus Pandemic on the 26th March 2020. He was 78 – just seven years older than me, but growing up as brothers with the small age gap. I decided to kick start it all just a few days later in the middle of this awful time which sees most of us under a form of 'house arrest' or self-isolation to give the official label.

Arthur was an inspiration, along with my family and friends who took me to the local Southampton dance halls back in the Fifties, giving me a taste of music and show-business. Little did I realise that these early days would set me on a life path, in which I would follow my dreams and make a living out of them. This precious photograph was taken in 1950, showing wonderful carefree days as we played in my grandfather's rabbit hutch area in the straw.

Arthur Marshall 1942 -2020

ACKNOWLEDGEMENTS

I am eternally grateful to several people across the decades, many of whom helped me along the path of life that I chose – or was chosen for me by a higher power? You will learn more about these special names as you read through each chapter, outlining the ever changing years in the music business. This life story is based in my home town of Southampton, being a wonderful place to grow up in, with so many memories that have thankfully stayed with me. Naturally, with the passage of time, we all have gaps in what we can still recall.

Part 1 of 'Southern Roots' covers the timescale from the mid Fifties up to 1972, when I decided to leave for a new life as a solo entertainer. This will later form the basis for another separate book that will take you up to the present day, plus more reminisces of international travel and famous names in show-business. The follow-up part 2 of SR will outline a wealth of local Hampshire groups, singers, DJs, managers with more information of the dance hall venues that saw people jiving the night away. Much of SR2 will be a spin-off from my website, including several pages full of rare photos and personal memories sent from all over the world by former entertainers who were part of the scene. I thank the following:

My parents John and Joan, family and friends
Arthur Marshall-Len Canham-Tony Cook-Reg Bicknell
Ted Vaughan-Ray Brewer-Johnny Dymond
The Beatles
My former band mates 1964-1972
Dave Sothcott-Glenn Lee-Mick Young-'Beau'- Geoff Baker
Eddie Harnett-Graham Medley-Steve Newman-Dave Bunney
Ronnie Allen-Derek Edmond-Ernie Fagg-Barry Morrow
Roy Cooper-Melvyn McCrea-Dave Maggs-Roy Perry-Tony Burnett
plus many more 'in-between' groups etc

FOREWORD

"Every time an old person dies – it's like a library burning down"

Alex Haley (author of Roots)

Everyone has a book inside them
I bet that has surprised many a proctologist!

David St John (author of Southern Roots)

Summer 2020 – ANNUS HORRIBILIS

This book has been in draft form for many years, as a spin-off from my personal website, originally set up as a means of publicising my profile as a professional comedy entertainer. The first (self-taught) effort was a basic one-page information layout with a photograph, as the new internet explosion was just around the corner back in 2005. My solo career had taken off in 1972, after enjoying the Swinging Sixties as lead singer for a few local pop groups around my home town of Southampton, then deciding to expand the site with more information. The title of 'Southern Roots' covers my early years of 1958-1972 in this wonderful world of entertainment, as well as receiving an incredible mini-encyclopaedia with the same title, posted from Australia. This forms part of the second book in this series, to be published later this year

The awful global Covid-19 pandemic has changed our lives forever, seeing billions of people isolated, forcing many of them to stay at home. It is a time to reflect on happier times, hence providing me with the opportunity to get my life story out there, in case my web-pages ever disappear. The enforced lockdown provided me with the free time to finalise this book, as well as being cathartic plus a way to alleviate any boredom, not thinking too much about the problems outside our four walls.

My first 'beat group' back in 1964 was a great bunch of young musicians, many of us being influenced by the chart-topping acts of that exciting era. In those days, we had the opportunity to see several big names on the 'package' shows that toured the theatres, following on from the old Variety days. Southampton boasted one of the finest venues in the shape of the Gaumont Cinema, later re-named the Mayflower in recognition of the Pilgrim Fathers who had stopped by in 1620, on their way to the New World. Three hundred odd years later saw the old town being pummelled by the Luftwaffe, due to having the strategic Docks as a main target. Post-war austerity slowly gave way to better times during the Fifties, with the new younger generation of 'baby boomers' enjoying a far nicer 'invasion' of American rock'n'roll acts. Most of these amazing new stars travelled by sea on the classic liners, carrying visiting Hollywood celebrities, in order to make appearances on television or on their own nationwide tours. Air travel for the masses was still on the horizon, so the lucky ones were able to spend a few days in pampered luxury as they crossed the Atlantic in style. This was also a boom time for the busy Docks, as ships filled every berth thus fuelling the local economy providing employment throughout the area.

My story goes back to the mid-Fifties, which saw a new kind of renaissance, imported from the USA. This enveloped me, so I always look back with gratitude to have been born in the right place and at the right time, growing up in the better years as the country was getting back on its feet after years of wartime misery. My original plan was to have published this book in 2018, celebrating sixty years on public stages, having started out as a ten year old rock'n'roll singer at the tender age of ten in 1958. However, work and other distractions seemed to have got in the way, as well as being commissioned to write the life story of another Southampton character. A well-known club owner from the Sixties had found my website, whilst searching on Southampton stories, being very impressed with the memories. You can read about his venue in Southern Roots – part 2, which follows the first section of my eventful life, as well as many stories of the local music scene, dance halls and the talented singers, groups, disc jockeys along with many more aspects of the good times for the lucky generation of that era.

I am very humbled at the positive feedback from my website ramblings over the last few years, then being asked if I could get it all down into book form. I was also approached by a professor at Southampton University in 2019, who was working on a project that encapsulated much of what I have been writing about. If you – dear reader – lived through these good old days, then I trust you will enjoy the nostalgia. Younger ones can hopefully get a taste of modern history that is rarely taught in schools.

We all have favourite songs that remain special throughout our lives, often from certain years. One of my favourites was a track from the 1965 Beatles album of 'Rubber Soul', mirroring a memorable year spent as part of a superb pop group - The Unforgiven. This Eastleigh-based band had the bonus of meeting new pals, who have remained mates since those heady days, with the exception of Eddie Harnett who is sadly no longer with us. He passed away in 2011 aged 63, having spent his last few years in Las Vegas. His good pal, ex band-mate Rick Champion was able to visit Ed in his final months, as well as being an important part of bringing him back to the UK with his ashes first being sent across to Ed's sister Jean in Florida.

Jean flew over from Florida to meet up with her sister Rosemary in Newbury, then travelling down to Southampton, to scatter Eddie's ashes at South Stoneham Garden of Rest on Tuesday 31st May. This tranquil spot is just a few yards from the nearby Ford factory, where our group had played several times in their Social Club. The rain stopped at the same time with some sunshine creeping through as if on cue. It was what Eddie would have wished for, enabling me to say a few words, sharing some memories of our great times all those years ago. I'm sure he was around us that day and still is......

I brought my guitar to sing a short burst of 'Just Like Eddie' (a hit by another local Eastleigh lad Heinz) the lyrics suiting what he was all about, so worth checking out. The final song fitted the occasion, a fitting musical farewell that Eddie would have wished for. John Lennon was the main writer of 'In My Life' being a reflective look back over his own early years, striking a chord with me as I have been writing about my own life in recent times. The words are perfect, as seen overleaf.

Eddie Harnett 2010

IN MY LIFE

There are places I remember
All my life, though some have changed
Some forever not for better
Some have gone and some remain
All these places have their moments
With lovers and friends I still can recall
Some are dead and some are living
In my life I've loved them all

But of all these friends and lovers
There is no one compares with you
And these memories lose their meaning
When I think of love as something new
Though I know I'll never lose affection
For people and things that went before
I know I'll often stop and think about them
In my life I love you more

Though I know I'll never lose affection
For people and things that went before
I know I'll often stop and think about them
In my life I love you more
In my life I love you more

Songwriters: John Lennon, Paul McCartney
In My Life lyrics © Sony/ATV Music Publishing LLC

x

IN THE BEGINNING

The first three words of the Bible seem like the best way to start my own story, as I look back over the decades that witnessed amazing developments and social changes. Librans are generally lucky people, seeing me join this club on the 12th October 1948 in the busy port of Southampton. The German bombers had naturally targeted this part of England during WW2, with heavy bombing raids on the docks. Many lives of brave merchant seamen were lost as the North Atlantic Convoys sailed from the USA, through the dangerous waters of the Atlantic Ocean. The enemy U-boats glided silently under the waves, determined to stop precious supplies reaching our shores. They also targeted the Woolston - based Supermarine factory, on the banks of the nearby River Itchen. Along with Castle Bromwich up in Birmingham, this building was turning out Spitfires - the planes that turned the tide of the war in 1940 as the Battle of Britain raged across the skies above the South East. Designer R.J. Mitchell had moved down from the Potteries, supervising the prototypes of this amazing aircraft, the first of which took off from Eastleigh airport in 1936. Mitchell sadly died in 1937, so never witnessed how his incredible skills changed history a few years later. He is much remembered as one of the city's most famous former residents, as well as some of his quotes:

"If anybody ever tells you anything about an aeroplane which is so bloody complicated you can't understand it, take it from me: it's all bollocks!"

R. J. Mitchell, advice given about his engineering staff to test pilot Jeffrey Quill during prototype trials.

Talking of status, I shared my first day on this earth along with Rick Parfitt, later finding fame as part one of my favourite groups who simply added Quo to their name. On that very same day, a young Luciano Pavarotti celebrated his thirteenth birthday, becoming another favourite artiste of mine as my musical tastes expanded year by year. Other Librans celebrated their birthdays around the same time as me, with the likes of two other major influences such as John Lennon and Cliff Richard. My father's birthday was on the 15th so always a happy

1

few days year after year. The war had ended some three years before my appearance on the world's stage, leaving the country in dire straits, austerity being a major issue. However, the defiant British people just got on with life, as they had done for many years before with a new optimism creeping in. 1948 also witnessed the birth of the NHS, as well as a new comprehensive system of education from which the new generation would benefit.

I was christened at Peartree Church, having a West Indian Godfather – Winston Cooper who was a great family friend. He was one of the so-called 'Windrush Generation from the late Forties, landing at Southampton instead of Tilbury. Winston was a very popular entertainer around the local pubs and clubs where he sang, having fun with the audiences as his personality shone through, and still remembered with affection from those days. In addition, he was one of the founding members of the West Indian Club, a major part of that community, integrating seamlessly in the neighbourhood. People of any race, colour or creed got on very well with each other as befits most port cities, so most of us youngsters were never really aware of any racial prejudice – if only life could be the same today.....

I was the only child of John and Joan, living at my grandparent's house in Manor Road Woolston, next to the railway bridge that overlooks the main Southampton to Portsmouth branch line. Later on, I had great fun in inviting new friends to come and look at my 'train set' at the bottom of the garden! This was the golden age of steam engines, watching these beautiful machines come thundering past, belching out the dark fumes with an accompanying whistle that could be heard all over the area. It was a large seven-bedroom home, with my grandparents running it as a boarding house, so we had a constant stream of crew members, who had docked in Southampton. From an early age, I was surrounded by a multicultural society with foreigners of all race, colour and creed who lodged at the family home so enjoyed hearing them talk in 'strange tongues' – this probably influenced me in later life, as far as learning a couple of languages plus gaining snatches of many more phrases. One long term lodger was known as 'Jimmy' Rahman from the former Aden (now Yemen) who taught me a few

Arabic words along with early lessons in chess, which came in useful a few years later when I played for my secondary school from 1960 on. Whilst rationing was still in force, I was never aware of any shortages in our household - probably due to the visiting merchant seamen bringing food in from their travels. I still recall eating bananas fresh from the West Indies which were a rare commodity back then!

I remember playing in the front garden, climbing through the ground floor window to join some African seamen who were sitting on the floor, whilst eating out of a pot with their fingers! Exotic dishes and far more tasty than some of the bland meals that formed the staple diet of those times. I called it 'jungle grub' as part of the experience. Apart from the food, I enjoyed listening to some of the strange new exciting music these visitors brought with them, as they played their latest records on our wind-up gramophone, being so different from the home-grown sounds that came from the radio at that time. These were early R&B, gospel, ska plus the new rock n roll that was taking off in the early to mid Fifties, so guess I was fairly lucky to have been 'weaned' on this music from such an early age. The Transatlantic crossings also meant that the sailors provided a steady supply of U.S. comics such as Dell and DC, many of which were sold to local shops. It was so exciting to read them from cover to cover as well as swapping them for a small part exchange price of a few pennies. The 1950s American way of life seemed so colourful, as the movies, music and amazing automobiles seemed a million miles away from the greyness of our own country. Jeans were also becoming very fashionable and affordable thanks to increased sales. Crew members bought loads of the much sought-after Wranglers and Levis in New York, then selling them to local clothes shops, who made a nice profit on these trendy jeans.

A similar movement was taking place in other busy UK ports as the visiting mariners imported these slices of American culture, mostly from the New York crossings. The most important of these cities was the northern port of Liverpool, some 250 miles to the North West, with a new breed of merchant seamen nicknamed the 'Cunard Yanks'. These seafarers mostly sailed on the much loved Queens Elizabeth, Mary and other liners within the same shipping line. They earned good money, coming home from many a trip, wearing the latest US fashions, bringing back the new hit records plus obscure early rock n roll records that would not be released in the UK for some while. All over the country, there would be teenage lads starting to form embryonic bands - especially up in Liverpool where a swaggering John Lennon would meet up with a young Paul McCartney on the 6th July 1957 at a school garden fete. The Quarrymen Skiffle Group (named after their Quarry Bank High School) soon evolved into a 'beat group' that conquered the world, as well as inspiring me to form my own band just after seeing them 'live' in 1963. These imported songs soon became part of many set-lists on Merseyside, as the young groups played them in their own style, the likes of which can be found on early albums by the Beatles and the like.

My parents were a great help to me as ours was a musical home, with a piano in the lounge, soon discovering that I had a natural ear for music, along with learning some guitar as well - the mid-Fifties 'skiffle' years also providing a chance to make music with a few pals. This was the usual back garden rehearsal with cheap guitars, washboard and the good old tea-chest with broom handle with one thick rope string that was plucked to provide a 'double bass' sound! Lonnie Donegan was the biggest star of this 'new' sound influenced by American Country, Blues, Folk and other styles. We must have made a racket but it was fun and a starting point for many of the great music stars that were discovering this great hobby, leading to many a dream come true. I was also telling jokes and doing silly stunts, including an impression of Toulouse Lautrec, after watching a film on our B&W television. 'Moulin Rouge' told the story of the famous diminutive French artist, whose paintings of the dancing girls at this world-famous Parisian nightspot captured the atmosphere. My family roared with laughter as I came back into the room, wearing a hat, makeshift walking cane, plus a small beard and shuffling slowly forward on my knees, which were shoved into my father's shoes. Entertainers love to be applauded, as well as having an all-important ego plus self-confidence on top of wanting to a make people happy. The seeds were being sown in a way that I could never have known, which leads me to repeating a gag from one of my all-time favourite comedians Bob Monkhouse, when looking back at his own beginnings as a child: *"I told my family that I wanted to be a comedian – they all laughed at me. They're not laughing now.."*

My father also played the accordion, encouraging me to knock out a few basic tunes on this massive instrument that I could only really handle whilst sitting down. The radio provided a non-stop selection of the current hits, although most of them were still firmly in the big band style until a certain Bill Haley and his Comets tore up the rule book in 1954. This ushered in the most exciting few years of what had been coined 'Rock and Roll' by American DJ Alan Freed, as the whole American culture swept in from across the Atlantic, with the UK slowly awaking from the legacy of war. People needed cheering up, with ballrooms packed as they danced the night away, with a new optimism that saw the rise of the new younger generation.

Thanks to my father, I was able to read and write when first starting infants school at the age of five as well as being interested in the world around me, this certainly helping me to absorb what was going on, although still too young to understand a lot of it. On most weekends, I used to take a trip over to the town centre on the old Floating Bridge which was a ferry service connecting both sides of Southampton across the River Itchen. It also offered a view of the Docks, filled with all types of ships which carried the rich and famous to our shores before the age of jet travel signalled the downturn of this luxurious way to cross the ocean to New York. It was quite safe for an eight year old lad to walk the streets alone at that time, being quite independent in many ways, so more than capable of enjoying the sights and sounds of this great port. My usual destinations were firstly the shops along St Mary's Street, which sold used American comics. These magazines were brought in by merchant seamen, offering a glimpse of an amazing world of luxury goods, massive cars and a lifestyle that was way ahead of our country at that time. We also enjoyed a taste of the USA when going to the movies, enjoying the Westerns plus classic cartoons along with the likes of Charlie Chaplin, Abbot and Costello, The Three Stooges, Laurel and Hardy plus science fiction films. Our local 'fleapit' was the Woolston Cinema on Portsmouth Road, just up the road from the Itchen Ferry terminal which linked us to the main city centre, before being replaced by the new bridge crossing in 1977. Saturday morning kids' shows were always fun, especially when able to let our pals in for free, by sneaking to the rear emergency doors, to allow the gatecrashers in. Quite noisy shows as well, whenever the projectors broke down or too long a delay in changing the film canisters, leading to cheers, whistles and stamping of feet.

1956 saw us move around the corner to the top of Garton Road. This three bedroom semi-detached house joined onto my Uncle Arthur's home, with the bonus of having the same railway line at the rear of our gardens. The purchase price was £1,000 at that time, but both parents were working over those early years so managed to cope with the mortgage and household bills. They were happy times as we ate well, with very few luxuries that today's generation have in excess – life was so much simpler then.

From a very early age, I had always enjoyed 'entertaining' the grown ups with my songs or party tricks, silly jokes and other gimmicks – I guess some might call it precocious, but I had no idea what that meant back then! My parents encouraged me in every way, sending me for piano lessons around the age of nine, but I soon got bored of learning notes and scales after a few lessons, as the music teacher soon discovered. She popped out of the room for a few minutes, then came hurrying back in a fluster as she heard me bashing out some heavy handed boogie-woogie style vamps on her beloved piano which didn't go down too well. I preferred Jerry Lee Lewis to Chopin so guess this was a sign that I was not cut out for a lifetime of classical influences, although loving all kinds of music. However, she gracefully informed my parents that I had a natural ear for music, so might as well just teach myself at home, this being the end of my early Elton John period! I do regret not keeping at it, but can still sit down at a keyboard and knock out any request thrown at me, although I mostly play the black notes and favourite key of F#. I later discovered that Irving Berlin only played in the same style/one key and it didn't really dent his song-writing career....Nor did it hinder Lennon and McCartney as they were not musically trained as such.

6

THE SILVER SCREEN AND A MUSIC MACHINE

The cinema was a great way to soak up the new breed of American movies, but I was too young to have seen some major films that had spearheaded a new way of life with the young. 1953 saw the release of 'The Wild One', starring Marlon Brando as the leader of a trouble-making motorcycle gang, causing mayhem wherever they went. His on-screen character of Johnny Strabler struck a chord with many a young lad who copied his look, with black leather jacket and jeans as well as some of the 'attitude'. Mildred's memorable quote from the film: *"Hey Johnny – what are you rebelling against?"* Johnny: *"Whaddya you got?"* The rival gang, led by actor Lee Marvin, went by the name of The Beetles – this was also used by an early version of the Beatles as the Silver Beetles before the final change, so they may have well been influenced by this? 1954 was the year that a minor hit single entered the US Billboard charts, but its significance was not felt until the next year when used on the soundtrack of the ground-breaking 'Blackboard Jungle'. Glenn Ford played the beleaguered teacher at a tough inner-city high school, faced with a classroom of juvenile delinquents - another new label that had crept in during these years. The violent scenes caused the movie to be banned in some states, the government trying to clamp down on this unruly influence, which naturally had the opposite effect. Throughout the movie, snatches of a catchy dance number grabbed the cinema audience, followed by the full song played over the end credits. This resulted in many youngsters jumping out of their seats to jive to the sounds of Bill Haley and the Comets version of 'Rock Around The Clock' in the aisles, much to the consternation of the management and staff who tried in vain to stop them. Fights broke out, leading to more bans in some states as the authorities were alarmed at these outbreaks of mass hysteria by a rebellious youth culture.

When this film was released in the UK, it had the same outcome, leading to more trouble across the country as mini-riots broke out when the music kicked in. One South London cinema saw gangs of Teddy Boys fighting with each other, slashing seats with flick knives or ripping them out of the floor to throw across the auditorium. Not all Teddy Boys (and Teddy Girls) were guilty of causing trouble, but the press naturally blew it all up, as this sold newspapers. The lads were merely enjoying the freedom of having money in their pockets, with employment booming in the post-war years, thus able to spend their wages on smart clothes and hit records. Traditionally garbed in long drape jackets with velvet collars, drainpipe trousers, 'brothel creeper' shoes or 'winkle-pickers' on their feet. Bootlace ties with long swept back hair smothered in Brylcreem, with the D.A. style at the back – the 'Duck's Arse' was also part of the cocky 'peacock' image.

It really was a start of a revolution and the feeling that the young were finally coming of age, enjoying new music, fashions and much more with each passing year. I was still at Ludlow Primary School, doing fairly well with the lessons, as well as making my fellow pupils and teachers laugh at some of my capers, although some of them got me into trouble. I wasn't a 'naughty' child as such, always cracking gags, with cheeky answers to some questions from our class teacher Mr Learmouth. One sticks out when I recall him asking us about what we would like to be when we grow up? My response? *"A Teddy Boy, Sir!"* Luckily, he smiled and quickly moved on, thus avoiding the chalk or blackboard rubber being thrown or the dreaded cane.

Sadly, my old school reports were lost many years ago, so I never had the chance to look back over them. Generally good comments on my educational efforts, mixed with a few negatives for being a bit of a non-conformist. Happy days, as most of us can look back at these precious times when life was basic but carefree. At least I have a few old photos to remind me of those times, as well as enjoying various Facebook pages full of other pupil's recollections, boosted by their own precious images

Thanks to the internet, it's been a massive game-changer, giving us the opportunity to keep in touch with former school mates and musicians. Science fiction of the Fifties has come true in many ways, as we can use our phones to have visual links all over the world, as well as watching videos of past performances on You Tube and the like.

1955 Ludlow School photo

Another 'teen' idol at this time was the great looking young James Dean, who only made three iconic movies – East of Eden, Rebel without a Cause and Giant, before being tragically killed in a car crash at the age of 24 in 1955. His persona was part of the whole movement that was changing our lives forever.

Bill Haley and his Comets may have spearheaded the advent of rock'n'roll, but this dance band leader was hardly the type of pop star that normally attract the girls. He was in his early Thirties at the time of his breakthrough successes, so quite 'old' as far as teenagers were concerned. Not the most handsome of pop stars, with chubby features and a silly 'kiss curl' that hung down from his thinning hair, so it all needed a new talent on the scene. A couple of years before this revolution kicked off, an 18 year old truck driver had walked into the legendary Sun Studio in Memphis Tennessee, in order to cut his first record. Elvis Presley had intended to surprise his mother with a 78 disc, but his amazing looks and unusual voice caught the attention of owner Sam Phillips. Within a short while, Elvis had recorded a few more songs, showcasing his vocal dexterity based on C&W, Gospel and new wave rock n roll that was sweeping the country. Many listeners thought he was a black performer at first, then mesmerised by his features and sexy stage movements that saw him appear waist up on prime-time US TV shows when finally breaking through! Elvis 'the Pelvis' shocked Middle America, soon becoming the New Saviour for the kids, as well as tearing up the rule book in the UK. Like many more young lads- my first 'idol'.

I only recall seeing odd clips of his early performances on our old B&W television, as well as listening to his first hits on an older lad's Dansette record player. By this time, my weekly walks over to the town centre were leading me to one of the many coffee bars that were springing up all over the place. The Milk Bar was situated in a terrace of shops on Hanover Buildings, a few yards down from the Medieval Bargate – the most prominent landmark dating from Norman times. The main attraction for me was one of the greatest inventions in the shape of a jukebox, holding stacks of 45s featuring the newest discs to make the U.K. charts, the likes of which were first published in 1952. The early hits were generally recorded by dance bands, singers and 'crooners', so quite tame at that time. This amazing machine was a Bal-Ami 40, that naturally held 40 discs, with a large selection wheel on the front that flipped the inside pages over, allowing the user to press the relevant button for the A or B side of the record. I didn't have that much pocket money to spend on drinks or play my favourite records, so relied on being cheeky, sitting right next to the jukebox, whereby the teenagers would often ask *"What do you want, Kid?"* in between choosing their own favourites.

The older youngsters put their three-penny bits into the slot, always asking me for any of my own selections as they know I would be singing along with the discs, so guess this is where my love of music really began. I was also glued to the way in which people put a coin in, then pressed the buttons which set this chrome-laden machine whirring away as it selected a chosen disc from a spinning rack, plopping it down onto the turntable. It was like a sci-fi robot with its flashing lights and loud volume, which is how the music needed to be heard!

Post-war Hanover Buildings (Source unknown)
The Milk Bar on the right

I was in heaven, as hit after hit was pumped out at a decent volume – much better than listening through small tinny speakers on a record player or radio. The café owner would often twig that the music was getting louder, as the volume control switch was on the back panel, allowing anyone to give a gradual tweak. He was often too busy serving coffees from the ubiquitous Italian Gaggia machine, so resorted to shouting at the culprit to turn it back down, with threats of pulling the plug on it. However, the non-stop music was bringing big profits into the small place, so the threats were rarely carried out. The most famous influential coffee bar had also opened in London, in Old Compton Street Soho, under the name of the "2 i's" It featured live music by skiffle groups, then followed by the new breed of young rock stars such as Tommy Steele, Cliff Richard and many more pioneers of the British music scene. These were soon spotted by recording companies, leading to great television shows such as '6-5 Special' and 'Oh Boy' launching more great careers. They were the first two major 'pop music' shows, later followed by 'Juke Box Jury,Top of the Pops, Ready Steady Go!' then the more highbrow show hosted by Bob Harris. 'The Old Grey Whistle Test' showcased the more progressive music ushered in by the early Seventies.

Many older music fans, lucky enough to be around in those days will often come up with the same answer to the stock question, when asked what was the first record that made an impact on them? The same for me, as it had to be the ground-breaking 1956 Elvis Presley hit of 'Heartbreak Hotel' with its great beat and hypnotic lyrics sang in the sexiest voice, laden with echo. The same year saw the cinema release of 'Rock Around The Clock', featuring more great rock tunes, followed by 'The Girl Can't Help It' starring Jayne Mansfield. This showcased the likes of Little Richard, Gene Vincent, The Platters and many more US singing stars that were now becoming well known on our side of the Big Pond. The Milk Bar jukebox was a big influence on me over a couple of years, realising that I knew most of the words, singing along with the likes of Buddy Holly, Jerry Lee Lewis, Eddie Cochran and many more. An even better way to hear these classic hits was when the travelling fairgrounds came to town, as they pitched up on the Common, off The Avenue, often staying for several weeks during the main summer holiday period. I headed straight for the Dodgems and other big rides that cranked up the atmosphere by playing the latest records through large sound systems. Hearing these tunes at high volume is a memory that has stayed with me across the years, as it has for many people who grew up listening to the soundtrack of their lives. The flashing lights also lifted the excitement levels as the sun went down.

My parents also took me along to the Grand Theatre, which stood opposite the Civic Centre in Southampton. This was a classic variety venue but suffering from the general downturn as the new medium of television was sweeping the country. It was later demolished, with the area becoming the main bus station for the Hants & Dorset Company (then known locally as 'Pants & Corset'). I loved watching all kinds of variety acts at this wonderful old theatre, including 'educational' glimpses of adult entertainment in the shape of the 'tableaux.' These strictly-regulated acts often consisted of the main curtains opening to reveal a mesh net curtain through which static nude and semi-nude ladies stood motionless in classic scenes of Roman temples and gardens etc. The gentle music played for a short while to enhance this 'artistic' display but within the confines of decency laws in place at that time! Quite an eye opener for a young lad but I thought it all quite amusing and more than titillating (excuse the pun), just carrying on enjoying all the singers, comedians, magicians and many more acts who trod those boards. I also loved the thrill of being invited onstage, whenever birthdays were mentioned getting a great kick out of being in the spotlight, allowing me to sing a quick verse or two of a favourite song. Just amazing to peer out through the spotlights to see people applauding me, so just another part of my ever growing desire to be in show-business.

My parents, Arthur and other family and friends also took me to nearby dance halls all over the area, allowing me to wallow in the atmosphere of the music played by top local bands such as Gil Hulme, Bert Osborne and many more traditional outfits. These were real musicians, reading off their scores, plus having great fun amongst themselves - a real camaraderie. I always stood at the front of the stage, watching how each band member played his/her instrument, as well as noting how the main lead singers at the front were attracting the most attention from the pretty ladies close by. They also made announcements in between the dances, which made for an entertaining evening plus having more variety with 'spot prizes' for the best dancers or any silly stuff.

I loved watching dancers of all ages having a great night out, jiving away for what seemed like hours and hours, with a really friendly atmosphere all around, apart from the odd punch-up that probably involved drinking too much mixed with jealousy etc! On several occasions, I was dragged onto the dance floor to join in with the gyrating crowd, especially on the bigger nights through Christmas plus the all-important New Year's Eve celebrations.

Naturally, I was not allowed to drink any alcohol at these places, apart from a few crafty sips of beer on the family table. Seeing people enjoying themselves and having so much fun seemed so right for me as a young kid. I wanted to be a part of it.

END OF THE PIER ACT!

In years gone by - this phrase was often used as a derogatory term for an older entertainer who might be past his - or her prime in show-business, ending up in some struggling variety show at the end of a crumbling pier. Ironically, it's a term that describes my first appearance at the age of ten, appearing in front of a large audience at a 'Teen Rock'n'Roll Dance Night' at one of the best-loved ballrooms in the South of England.

There were many local dance halls around Southampton during these boom times, offering a great night out as people of all ages preferred to jive, than waltz around the floor to the sounds of the older established traditional bands. One of the most popular ballrooms was situated at the end of the Royal Pier, opened in 1833 by a young Princess Victoria, who often sailed across to the Isle of Wight throughout her long rein as Queen from 1837-1901. Osborne House on East Cowes was her favourite home away from London and Windsor, so having fond memories of Southampton when passing through. Back on April 10th 1912, the whole Pier was packed as onlookers gasped at one of the most magnificent liners ever built slowly glide out of its berth, on its way to a tragic end - the Titanic. She sailed from berths 43/44 in the Old Docks about half a mile away, but would have been seen by those crammed onto the Royal Pier as she steamed down Southampton Water into the Solent, then onto the watery grave that lay undiscovered until 1985.

Sadly, only the façade of the beautiful entrance hall building remains as a preserved landmark in the city. This followed years of neglect as the old Pavilion Ballroom suffered from two major fires back in the 1980s. The derelict jetty and rusty remains of the old structure constitute a major eyesore to the visiting passengers on many cruise ships as they sail into the New Docks, hardly the best of welcomes to one of the most famous harbours in the world.

Royal Pier 1950s

The classic gatehouse building dates from the 1930s, being recently renovated by a local Asian restaurant owner, now used as a favourite dining venue after being closed for many years. Some early critics labelled it as 'the Wedding Cake' but it has stood the test of time as one of the city's most loved buildings.

Late 1958 was an exciting time for me as a ten year old, but I never imagined what the future held for me as I prepared for my first real public performance. My mother Joan worked part time in the café at the Royal Pier, getting on really well with the manager, a flamboyant 'camp' promoter by the name of Len Canham, who was rapidly gaining much respect, knowing what kind of music would pull in the crowds. She kept pestering Len to give me a chance on one of the new 'Teen Dance' nights, to allow me to sing some of the Top Ten hits of the day, so he finally agreed to feature me as a 'Mystery Guest - with a difference.' I was really excited about my show later that evening, as it was going to be rather special in more ways that I could ever have imagined. It didn't take me too long to decide on dark blue denim jeans, a natty white shirt with upturned collar. My hair was rather long with a floppy fringe that set off my cheeky face - so everybody kept telling me! I was looking forward to a great night out and had been practising a few of my favourite songs by singing along with the records on the café jukeboxes or when they played on the radio.

To reach the venue entailed a ten minute walk down the hill from our Woolston home, then onto the old Floating Bridge ferry for a short ride, with another thirty minute walk to the dance hall, unless a bus was needed if raining or too cold! My parents and a few relatives were in tow, so we had the usual laughs and sing-along, as we made our way to one of Southampton's most popular music venues, which was usually packed most nights. The Royal Pier Pavilion Ballroom stood at the end of the long wooden walkway, which was one of England's most well known piers until falling into disrepair throughout the 1980s onwards. Many of the girls had to negotiate the wooden slats that often led to their stiletto heels getting caught in the gaps, or even broken off on their way to and fro.

Royal Pier Teenagers' Party Night

The pier offered a great view of Southampton docks as well as offering amusement arcades, tearooms with the ballroom - always a popular meeting place for thousands of people over the years. There is talk of a massive regeneration plan that might see the whole structure restored to its former glory, leading to a new generation of dancers walking along the boards to enjoy a taste of Southampton's old nightlife? Many locals met their future spouses at this popular ballroom as this really was the best 'hop' in town, with the perfect atmosphere in which to chat each other up.

We reached the entrance hall, proceeding to the ticket desk, whereby a steward ushered us through a side door, as I was a guest 'artiste' so the paying customers didn't seem too bothered – some wag even *shouted "Eh Nipper – can we have your autograph?"* I must explain that 'nipper' or 'mush' is a common name for any local lad and can still be heard to this day, although you will hear rather stronger names from any Pompey FC supporters a few miles to the east! This appearance came about, thanks to my proud mum who always supported and encouraged me, but not in a 'pushy' way as seen in many 'stage mothers'.

Royal Pier Pavilion Ballroom (Mecca days)
Photo courtesy Johnny Dymond – resident 60s DJ

We walked through the doors to be met with a fantastic hot noisy atmosphere, with hundreds of teenagers bopping away to the non-stop beat of the group onstage. The resident band on this particular night was The Three Stars, comprising of drummer Brian 'Fergy' Ferguson, plus Alan Fraser on double bass, with lead guitarist and vocalist Johnny Watson. John later switched to drums – one of the best in the business, as well as working in Hamburg with several bands during the early Sixties. In 1962 John struck lucky by backing Gene Vincent and other big names, later being approached by a bunch of scruffy musicians who were looking to replace their own drummer Pete Best, but JW turned them down. I recently had a wonderful message from Gill Richards, who had been going out with Johnny around this time, so knew quite a lot of what went on over there. The Beatles had been sharing the bill at the same club as Rory Storm and the Hurricanes, whose own drummer Ringo Starr often deputised for Pete when not around. John and Paul were looking to ditch Pete Best for a number of reasons, making discreet approaches to JW.

Apart from earning decent money in the main clubs, J.W. was reluctant to accept this new offer, partly due to not approving of John Lennon's behaviour towards the 'working' girls on Herbert Strasse within the notorious Reeperbahn, the heart of Hamburg's 'Red Light' district. Lennon had a misogynist side to him, possibly due to a dysfunctional upbringing, not helped by the tragic death of his mother Julia who was knocked down in the road close to John's Aunt Mimi's house, where he was being raised. JW suggested that perhaps the Beatles might look at recruiting Ringo instead. Johnny was a better drummer than Ringo, even giving him a few lessons to adapt to the new group's style. JW also knew that there was only one strong personality in the Beatles, which would have resulted in major clashes. I think you know the rest of the story.

I went backstage to meet Len Canham, who really made me very welcome with a pep talk, telling me how important this show might be for me! He was rather surprised at my lack of nerves, as I had never appeared in front of so many people before, but I guess that I had an inbuilt confidence, although I sometimes get the odd butterflies before certain shows. The Three Stars finished their first set, before coming backstage to meet me, then quickly running through a few possible songs as I had not had the chance for a proper rehearsal, but these lads could play anything. Johnny picked up his guitar, making notes of the titles and keys, trying each song in turn, with me starting off with Johnny finding my pitch and a basic arrangement - in other words we 'busked' it! Armed with my short set-list, the group went back onstage for a few more numbers before a roll of the drums, then introducing me as the 'surprise' of the night! The music played me on, as I practically ran onto the stage with the glare of the spotlights blinding me for a few seconds, not letting me see where all the applause and even a few screams were coming from! Everybody stopped dancing and faced the stage to see what was going on to discover the 'surprise' of the night!

Royal Pier Ballroom 1958

John played a chord for my cue, launching into one of the most famous opening lines of all time *"A wop bop a lula - a wop bam boom...."* tearing through this rock and roll classic of Little Richard's 'Tutti Frutti' which got the crowd clapping along and joining in with me. I was too young, as were most of the audiences back then, to realise that the title of this song was a euphemism for a gay man, when originally penned by Little Richard, a flamboyant homosexual, as well as being a favourite ice cream! The original bawdy lyrics had been cleaned up for its release to the general public, becoming a massive hit. This amazing talent died in May 2020, the sad loss of another pioneer in rock'n'roll with his whooping hollering vocals, stage antics, pounding the piano keys like a dervish, mostly standing up. His hits formed part of the Beatles' early repertoire, ideally suited to Paul's vocal talents on such memorable tracks such as 'Long Tall Sally' and the like.

I finished the song, overwhelmed with the feedback from the audience, the memory of which has stayed with me ever since. I carried on with a few more songs such as "Rock Around the Clock,

24

Jailhouse Rock" and a C&W flavoured hit "I Traced Her Little Footprints in the Snow" before taking my bow and running backstage to cool down after this amazing experience.

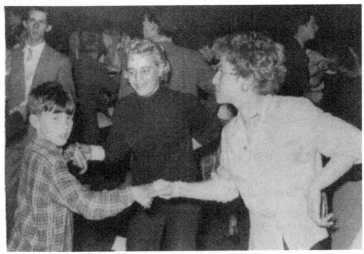

Jiving with my Teddy Girl fans!
Sisters Janet and Barbara Appleton

I was hooked, vowing to make a career out of this when I left school a few years down the line, little knowing that my young dreams would carry on long after this time of my life. Len was really pleased with my debut, paying me in boxes of chocolates and Coca Cola, as well as rebooking me at the Pier and a couple of other local venues. One being the Peartree Hall on the corner of Upper Vicarage/Garton Roads, just a few yards down from our new home at the top of the road, having moved there in 1956. The hall and surrounding houses were later demolished to make way for the toll booths on the Woolston side of the new Itchen Bridge. The large Eastleigh Town Hall featured popular Teen Dances, so another favourite of mine until this early 'career' took a turn for the worse. One of the newest solo rock'n'roll singers was also making his debut in the area, billed as 'South Africa's Elvis' but a few years older than me. He was a great entertainer, becoming firmly established over the next few years by fronting his own groups until just a few years ago. Little did he know that I would be taking over his role some ten years later, by replacing him in my last pop group in 1968.

None of us were fully aware that children were not allowed to perform in licensed premises if under the age of twelve at that time, so within a short time the school authorities got in touch with my parents, as the word had got around. So, dear reader, I have to tell you that I had to 'retire' from show-business at the tender age of ten! Gutted, but determined to keep at it for a while, limiting my vocal outings whenever the family went out to local pubs. Many a 'boozer' had a resident piano player who would invite singers up on a 'free and easy' night, trying hard to accompany those that could murder any song going in between the better ones! This was an early version of karaoke providing me with a chance to try different songs, although many an old fashioned musician had no idea of the latest hit tunes that I was offering up.

After the 'New Renaissance' of popular music in the mid to late Fifties, the whole scene died off for a couple of years – some often quote Buddy Holly's tragic death as *'The Day the Music Died'*, quoted in Don McClean's 1971 'American Pie'. The formerly outrageous Little Richard had flipped his lid, choosing a religious way of life for the next few years, as well as Jerry Lee Lewis suffering a media backlash when bringing his new young bride to England for a 1958 tour. It emerged that she was only thirteen and a distant cousin, although their (short-lived) marriage was legal in their US state. Lewis was twenty two at the time, having been married twice before, so the tour was cancelled, with his career going into freefall back home in the USA. From around 1960 to 1962 the UK charts were dominated by rather 'tame' US singers such as Bobby Vee, Brian Hyland, Tommy Roe and similar safe 'boy next door' types. Even Elvis lost his way during that era, due to his manager sidelining The King into a conveyor-belt line of bad movies, some of which produced decent hits but at the loss of his credibility. Apart from ripping his protégé off for millions of dollars, Colonel Tom Parker – a former fairground huckster, deprived the world of seeing Presley in concert, due to the fact that he was an illegal immigrant without a U.S. passport.

Presley had influenced the likes of our home-grown successes such as Cliff Richard, Billy Fury and others who kept up a decent run of big new phases creeping in. Hank Marvin was also the proud owner of the first red Stratocaster in the UK, Cliff having ordered it from the USA.

I still possess that original vinyl 45 rpm disc, being the first record I ever bought with my pocket money, boosted by helping out with an older lad's newspaper round. Popular classical music also featured in my tastes at that age, thanks to my father who loved the genre of opera amongst his own favourite listening. Another vivid memory was being taken to the Gaumont theatre, to enjoy an evening of ballet, with a dual bill of Delibes' 'Coppelia' and 'Les Sylphides' so having quite an impact on me. Our local Woolston record shop was Spikins Electrical, on the Colonnade, mainly selling white goods, later branching out with selling discs. It was so good rummaging through the varied record boxes, taking the disc to the counter in order to have it placed on a turntable, piped through to the listening booths. The assistants turned a blind eye to the likes of us young ones, not being the most spending types, so I thank them for allowing me to soak up the new hits as they were released. It made the shop look busy, attracting more paying customers.

Spikin Records – the days of the 78s

Eyebrows were raised when I chose 'Move It' for that all important first purchase, followed by picking out an E.P. (extended play) 45 rpm recording of Tchaikovsky's '1812 Overture' with its wonderful melodies before exploding into the finale with rousing climax of cannons and bells - to my ears, this was also rock'n'roll!

Move It 1958 – my first 45

Dorothy ran a small printing company, producing most of their publicity, amongst many other duties that helped to boost the business. She really was the power behind the throne, keeping Reg in check whenever he drummed up new madcap ways to publicise his growing bunch of musicians. The Calvert 'Empire' had also spread to the Midlands, by running nearly thirty dance halls in the area, so it was time for another move. Reg was like a father figure to his band of modern day wandering minstrels, being fiercely protective of them. They all respected him as a friend and a fair manager who made sure they had good wages, as well as decent accommodation, transport plus good amplification equipment and speakers that were needed for the larger venues. This was completely different to most managers and agents, many of them being unscrupulous people then and now, as the history books can show.

1960 Reg with a room full of talent!

Photograph by kind permission of Susan Moore-personal collection
Len Canham's unwelcome attention to some of Reg's artistes, as they got changed backstage, gave cause for concern, but this was soon nipped in the bud when Reg had stern words with him. It stopped right there. Another problem arose as the militant Musicians Union were attempting to enforce a closed shop in the dance halls, in which only paid-up members would be allowed to play. This was all part of the traditional dance band musicians' annoyance, looking down on these new young upstarts who threatened their livelihoods as rock'n'roll was sweeping out the old guard.

In 1961 they discovered a beautiful large country house near Rugby, by the name of Clifton Hall, also looking good on the new business cards. Within a very short time, the house and garden were full of new young pop groups, practising their skills day and night, as well as letting off mild steam as any teenagers do. The Calverts kept a tight rein on the lads, making sure that none of them fell by the wayside with many of the temptations that surrounded the music business then – and now. It was like one big happy family and the best years of their lives.

The local press and media soon latched onto this unique 'music academy' which they then labelled 'The School of Rock'N'Roll'. It also produced the fledgling members of the Fortunes, Rocking Berries, Pinkerton's Assorted Colours, with later chart successes. Shortly after this big change, Reg then took on a flamboyant character, whose horror-based Jack The Ripper act was shocking audiences all over the UK. David 'Screaming Lord' Sutch, with the guidance and marketing skills of the Calverts, was making the front pages with his outrageous publicity stunts. 1964 was the next venture due to the rise of 'pirate radio', beamed from old ships moored outside of the UK in international waters, thus falling out of UK legislation. Radio Caroline was the first station, employing young trendy DJs, many of whom would become household names after the government closed them all down in 1967. The staid BBC was losing its grip on youth culture, despite its flagship Top of the Pops, thus opening the floodgates of the best music around, presented by young irreverent cheeky presenters.

This set the wheels in motion, seeing Reg and David decide to start their own 'pirate' radio station as a publicity stunt. Reg came across Shivering Sands, a set of abandoned WW2 defence towers out in the Thames Estuary. Radio Sutch started transmitting for a short period, before David returned to performing his live shows back on the mainland. Reg continued, changing the name to Radio City, putting the station on a professional footing. His own broadcasts were very successful, with his natural flair stemming from his earlier disc jockey days back on the Southampton ballroom circuit. His gift of the gab and superb record collection made for popular listening.

36

Reg and Dorothy Calvert – all at sea!
Photograph by kind permission of Susan Moore

This whole story had a tragic ending in 1966, when Reg was shot by the former Chairman of Radio Atlanta/Caroline South, who had hijacked Radio City, then blackmailed Reg for 50% of the profits and £5,000. In one of the worst miscarriages of justice, Oliver Smedley was charged with murder, then reduced to manslaughter, but acquitted to everybody's amazement. He claimed 'self defence' as well as all the witnesses on Reg's side being cancelled at the hearing. A 'D' notice was issued, banning the press and media from reporting on the case notes, which were then under lock and key until 2000, before released for public inspection at the National Archives in Kew. It was a massive Establishment cover-up, in which Reg was used as a scapegoat as the authorities were intent on closing all loopholes in the Marine Broadcasting Act, followed by the demise of the pirate radio ships. There were criminal undercurrents in the industry anyway, but this case fuelled the paranoia as well as conveniently paving the way for the BBC to introduce Radio One in 1967. Many of the former pirate D.J.s were then legitimised, moving onto new pastures but denying youngsters the means to enjoy the right kind of music in a contemporary fashion.

Reg Calvert was an amazing man, well ahead of his time until having his life cut short in this tragic way, leaving his devoted wife

Dorothy to pick up the pieces for a short while, as well as looking after their young daughters. She was a tough clever woman, with a great brain, complementing Reg's success over the golden years as well as being fondly remembered as a 'mother' figure to the many talented youngsters that were all part of the story. Fast forward a few years, as I managed to get in touch with Susan (Calvert) Moore, living just a few miles from the old Clifton Hall. She is a very talented portrait artiste, silk painter and writer, having published a recent trilogy of books that tells the incredible story of her much-missed father. 'Life and Death of a Pirate' covers the years that saw Reg's talents and foresight explode into his pipe dream of the School of Rock'n'Roll, much copied by later managements, also mirrored in the movie industry. Other authors have written parts of the Calvert story but with many inaccuracies, so best ignored. This is the <u>official</u> version from the inside – a fascinating account. Susan originally wrote it all as a stage play, which had rave reviews when staged around the country, but was then persuaded to expand it into published book form. The big names of Parnes, Epstein, Stigwood, Loog-Oldham and other Sixties impresarios made the headlines back in the day, but the name of Reg Calvert should have been up there with them all, if he hadn't had his life cut short. Maybe some perceptive television production company might pick up on it all, as it makes for a very successful documentary. Take a look at Susan's website for more information:

www.susan-moore.co.uk

of three major chords, which made it all a lot easier back in the day. My basic knowledge of reading music came in useful, as a legacy of my previous piano lessons, then being revived a few years later when learning a new skill of writing out my own musical arrangements. This was all to be useful in my later solo career, in the days of the club scene, accompanied by backing musicians. As this particular book is concentrating on my early entertainment period, I intend to write a fresh one that covers the times after leaving the pop group scene in 1972.

October 1962 was another milestone when hearing the most amazing record on the radio. Many of us listened under the bedclothes on our new-fangled transistor radios, tuned into Radio Luxembourg on 208 Medium Wave. Not the best of signals, fading in and out, but giving us more variety with the best hits of the era. I still laugh at the adverts, including a 'miracle' way of winning the Football Pools of the time. Gambling expert Horace Batchelor plugged his *"Famous Infra-Draw Method"* promising a fast track way to massive cash jackpots, simply by writing off to a small village situated on the outskirts of Bristol, spelt out *"K.E.Y.N.S.H.A.M."* as many will recall!

This unique catchy record reminded me of the Bruce Chanel hit 'Hey Baby' from a few months, before as a lilting harmonica riff led into this new group singing in great harmony. There was something about the whole sound that stood apart from other releases. 'Love Me Do' by this new Liverpool group was to open the floodgates for fledgling bands across the country, with the Mersey Sound conquering the world, as well as putting the 'Great' back into Great Britain. It signalled the end for the mostly American musical greats that had dominated the UK charts with rather insipid crooners along with Elvis, who was suffering due to his constant stream of conveyor belt movies and soundtrack releases. Since my first public performances had been curtailed, I still went on family trips to nearby pubs and clubs, giving me the chance to get up to sing any current hit of the day.

The Beatles inspired a whole new generation of 'beat groups' as they were known, prompting me to come out of my enforced 'retirement' by later joining a few different line-ups of musically minded pals. I was also lucky enough to have seen the 'Moptops' in action during 1963, as they played two separate tours that year, appearing at the Gaumont. The tour was originally advertised as the Roy Orbison Show, so I really wanted to see him anyway, being another firm favourite of mine. The word soon got around that a new 'supporting' act was now added to the bill, following on from previous tours with Helen Shapiro and the dual-billed Tommy Roe/Chris Montez Show, all of whom were very annoyed at the demoting of the advertised top of the bill artistes! A new word was coined as 'Beatlemania' gathered momentum, followed by more of the 'Merseybeat' groups, plus many more fanning out to the rest of the country. The main cities led this vanguard with Manchester, Birmingham, London and others paving the way for the imminent 'Brit Invasion' crossing the Atlantic to conquer the USA in 1964. Oddly enough, our own city never matched these other musical hotspots, despite having several top notch professional groups.

This show was scheduled for May 1963, with advance tickets being sold a few weeks before on a Monday morning. The last few weeks of that record-breaking cold winter were slowly fading away, following sub-zero temperatures, heavy snow and general chaos that made life difficult for the country. Ken Derham - one of my best school pals was also enamoured with the Beatles, so we decided to join the ever-growing queue of fans, queuing down the side of the theatre. Ken arrived on the Sunday afternoon, in readiness for the front box office opening. These days, most live concerts have been ruined by the greedy touts and unscrupulous companies that use the internet to harvest the best seats. Then sell at inflated prices to the detriment of the real fans, so things were far less complicated during those early years. He grabbed a good spot on the alleyway, leading down to the rear car park. Within a short time, the whole place was full of excited kids with sleeping bags, blankets, food and drink, much of which was replenished by family and friends throughout the day and night. Later on, as the darkness drew in, it was my turn to take over this precious spot, soaking up the buzz of anticipation. It really was a 'feel-good' time, all of us being aware of being part in a new movement, but still being a little scared at the prospect of nuclear war that might have

44

wiped us all off the planet. The Cuban Missile crisis of 1961 had raised tensions in the Cold War, which saw the Russians and Americans facing off, each of them threatening to utilise their advanced weaponry in a long drawn arguments at the United Nations. We all sighed with relief as the escalation gradually slipped away, leaving us with a hope for peace in the years to come. The JFK assassination in November had also worried the world.

Ken   David

Throughout the cold night, we all chatted to each other with outbreaks of Beatles' songs from their first LP as 'Please Please Me' had been released in March. I still have my original copy – the Mono version that commands very high prices when sold on EBay and other outlets. I need to dig it out of my loft to check the label, due to the first pressings being very rare, often selling for a few thousand pounds! Likewise, I have a near-complete collection of the Beatles Magazine, published by the official fan club so maybe time to cash in? Monday morning crept in, as we counted the hours until able to stand up, stretch legs then slowly make our way to the box office in an orderly way. No pushing, shoving or being overtaken, unlike many other queues that make the headlines. As it was a school day, I naturally went home with the blessing of my parents, who wrote out a covering letter to explain my absence, due to a 'heavy cold'. If I had been found out, then it would have been worth a caning, as this punishment occasionally came my way for fairly mild reasons.

Beatles 1963 Booking Form

Note the ticket price of 10/6d in old money, which is about £9 at 2020 calculations! Not bad value to attend such an historical show, but none of this passed our minds at that time as we were too busy soaking it all up. I'm sure that many of us have laughed at the memory of the time when Brian Epstein was touting his new group around the London record companies in 1962. An audition at the Decca studios resulted in one of the most memorable quotes in pop music history, as A&R man Dick Rowe turned them down with a farewell saying: *"Sorry lads, but guitar group are on the way out...."* He actually denied this for the rest of his life, blaming the other executives for this biggest mistake in the business, although Epstein validated it in his official autobiography.

The eagerly anticipated Monday 20th May came around, to see us two fans travelling across town in good time to catch the first house, as these shows were still based on the old variety theatre days, often with a comedian/compere to run the night. They also warmed the audiences up, introducing each act with teasing them on the way, hinting that the *"four lads were just behind the stage curtains",* as they swayed a little. The polite fans actually kept quiet for most of the show, offering Roy

Orbison the chance to weave his magic with his dramatic ballads, but later getting noisy and restless as we could not wait to see our new 'idols' in the flesh. The decibels hit the roof as the curtains rose to reveal the four most famous people of that year.

It was the most incredible atmosphere with non-stop screaming throughout their set, which was difficult to hear as they only used small amplifiers through the basic house system! I recall John and George using Vox AC 30 amplifiers with Paul playing his Hofner 'Violin' bass guitar through a Vox T60 set-up - not forgetting Ringo bashing away on his Ludwig Classic drum set. Like many a young lad across the country, this was a pivotal moment for me as it inspired me to get serious about forming a real group and emulating my new found heroes. I guess you could call it an 'epiphany' by setting me on a new course in life, the likes of which I never envisaged at that age. Upon discovering that I could play harmonica a few years before being heavily featured on the new blues hit records, my Grammar School pals laughingly reminded me that I attracted a small group of girls in the play areas by knocking out the opening riff of 'Love Me Do'. My hair was also getting longer due to these influences all around me, leading to a few altercations with some of the more conservative teachers. I was also rather outspoken at times, when querying certain lessons, leading to more reprimands. My studies were fairly good, with adequate exam results across all subjects, but I seemed to learn much more outside of my school time by reading about subjects that I was interested in. English Language and French were my favourite lesson, the latter staying with me ever since, so always get to practice the language whenever hearing anybody speak it – even complete strangers in the street! Unlike other pals, I was never tempted to start smoking, but confess to buying packets of French cigarettes to impress the visiting foreign students who visited the town on summer trips. Southampton is twinned with Le Havre, just across the Channel, so I used to stroll nonchalantly near the ferry terminals, fake-puffing on a Gauloise, hoping to chat up the odd girl in her native language. Not always successful as they mostly stayed in groups, accompanied by protective teachers or too many lads, often seeing me walk straight past! I thought I was being 'cool' but they didn't.

Later that same year, another incredible package tour was announced, starring the Everly Brothers and Bo Diddley, with an added attraction of another new group that were causing a great deal of controversy amongst the older generation. Completely different from the Beatles, sporting even longer hair plus 'attitude', as well as spearheading the burgeoning R&B style of Chuck Berry, Muddy Waters, John Lee Hooker and many more. The Rolling Stones, like the Beatles, attracted both boys and girls for different reasons, forming part of a 'rebellion' as they were shrugging off the restraints of their parents. This rejection of old values happened in the mid Fifties, but this was even newer on a much bigger scale with an onslaught of fresh talent plus a chart full of amazing hits. The Stones were my second big influence in 1963, partly thanks to a Lennon & McCartney composition of 'I Wanna Be Your Man' that saw Jagger & co enter the charts for the second time in that year, following their first unique release of a Chuck Berry song. 'Come On' was a superb record, aided by clever PR by their management promoting them as 'the bad boys of pop', which naturally gained massive press attention. The reaction of the fans was electric on this latest show, as well as giving me some ideas of my own, due to these two new leviathans of music setting my life's template, embracing both of their styles. I ploughed on with my quest to form my own group for a few months to no avail as I could not latch onto a few of my pals who were also on the same new path.

The Beatles second tour of 1963 was announced for the December show, the overwhelming demand for these precious tickets saw me losing out on a chance to obtain a decent seat. Relegated to the Upper Circle- the 'Gods' still provided me with a second chance to see my idols yet again, but very difficult to actually hear them above the non-stop screams! I also attracted some admiring glances, due to wearing my black corduroy Beatle suit with matching Chelsea boots, so all part of the fun. Like most 'beat groups' we bought our fancy stage clothes from 'The Shirt King' at the top of St Mary's Street- the 'In Place' for all kinds of fancy gear.

Peter Phillips in my borrowed suit

Wish I had a photo of this outfit, but here is my childhood pal Pete Phillips, sporting it whilst standing in a dustbin in our back garden at Garton Road! You can just make out the Anderson Shelter on the right, which was used as an air raid shelter in WW2, then put to more peaceful use as a post-war garden shed. Across the railway line from my grandparents' old house, which cannot be seen these days due to massive trees that cover the main building. Note the reversed Churchillian V-sign.....

THE ABDO-MEN 1964

At last – my first real group after a few months of trying to find like-minded individuals. Not really sure how we all met up, but it worked out very well as the line-up clicked in. The pun-name came about as they were looking for a catchy label, by opening a dictionary at the first page, landing on this word! Dave Sothcott played lead guitar and vocals, alongside drummer Glenn Lee, bass guitarist Geoff Baker plus another guitarist Mick Young, a young London lad who was staying at the YMCA for a while. Dave lived locally, often calling by to watch me sing and play piano, leading to an invitation to join his existing group. Glenn's first job was as a 'butchers' boy' for a local shop, giving him the opportunity to take the firm's delivery motorbike home for the night and weekend. The fitted sidecar allowed him to load his small drum kit in readiness for gigs and rehearsal sessions, but left the smell of meat on his gear! He joked that his first full day in the shop was spent by trying to hang up the mincemeat!

Our musical tastes were all the same, setting about with practising a repertoire of mixed songs drawn from old rock'n'roll tracks with recent Beatles and Stones numbers. Having discovered being able to play blues harmonica, with note-bending, added to the R&B numbers, enabling us to include many of these new hits that were covered by emerging UK chart bands. Chuck Berry, John Lee Hooker, Sonny Boy Willamson, Bo Diddley and many more of these great talents inspired us to scrape up a decent programme in a very short time. I added maracas and tambourine, copying Mick Jagger to some extent, although he had naturally copied the American acts, with his moves, especially James Brown when the Stones were touring America.

Early practices took place at a variety of family front rooms, then managing to secure the use of a third floor room above a tailor shop in St Mary Street, opposite the legendary Henrys Records - the main disc outlet for many years. For some reason, we drafted in a good-looking long-haired guy who played the organ, but in a very basic one-fingered style. It didn't really work out, so we politely suggested that he might wish to try another new group. Dave recalls that he took it bad, even threatening to commit suicide over this dismissal! Mick 'the Cockney' moved on, leaving a gap to fill, which was another lucky moment of my life as a future lifelong friend joined us on rhythm guitar-a gold coloured Harmony. Known as 'Beau' with an amazing high voice range that augmented our music to include Beach Boys and Four Seasons hits of that time, he would later switch to bass guitar, having great success including a recording career, as well as being a lifelong mate. This new input came about as Dave Sothcott's mother had a doorstep round, taking weekly payments for some business venture, bringing her in contact with Beau's household. They got chatting about their respective pride in their sons, which then led to the musical link. Beau slotted in like a dream, elevating our sound to a higher level as we had so much fun in between knocking the new songs into shape.

The Sothcotts moved to Shirley, as a base for their dry-cleaning/laundry business, with Dave's father Ron running a small garage repair centre on the corner of Clovelly and St Marys Roads. Situated just across the street was the massive Territorial Army Centre, becoming our new practise hall, with wonderful acoustics, making us sound even better. Our first paid gigs were at this T.A. Drill Hall, with a small door charge that saw a decent number of new fans coming to watch us. We were also booked for small birthday parties, wedding receptions as well as branching out to local pubs, youth clubs, schools etc. Ron was our (unpaid) manager/roadie, as we travelled to shows in family cars or even buses if not far from home, so all part of the fun at the time. We eventually progressed to an old Bedford Dormobile - a firm favourite bandwagon during the Sixties. Other popular makes were the Commer, J4 then the ultimate (expensive) new van, manufactured in Southampton – the magnificent Ford Transit.

Whilst Liverpool had its own Cavern Club, we were lucky to have our own smaller version situated down the stairs leading to the Kasbah Coffee Bar, on the corner of London and Ordnance Road. This was the most popular meeting spot in town, being owned at one time by Brian 'Kiwi' Adamson, the owner of the prestigious Silhouette Club in St Michael's Square. You may be aware that I have published his biography on Amazon books – an amazing story outlining his many years living the life of a playboy, gambler, womaniser and world traveller. The place attracted local bikers at first, before the new wave

51

of 'Mods' took over, with the side street full of flashy Lambrettas and Vespas, adorned with cascades of mirrors, headlights and all manner of customised scooters parked all along the road.

Local neighbours naturally complained about the noisy gatherings in the street, leading to the Kasbah having to close early or cut the opening hours. Upon entering the front door, the kids walked down the staircase, leading to the main bar, with the jukebox playing non-stop hits throughout the day and evening. Next to the counter was a door that took you into a small cellar that had been cleared out in order to provide the area for bands to play. Very cramped, but us early 60s groups only had small basic sound equipment, so able to set up to entertain the crowd listening in the main room, plus a few brave souls who squeezed into the cellar to stand right in front of us. No problems – especially mostly being gorgeous 'chicks' as we called them back then. Singing with bands was also one of the reasons that many of us made good use of it, allowing us to chat up our new fans- or 'groupies'.

The drummer and guitarists had their own amplifiers, with our p.a. amp being an Italian Meazzi, about the size of an old 80s VHS video recorder, standing on four metal legs. Low output and plugging in a couple of Reslo Ribbon microphones, being the most popular models for many bands. Another popular amp was the Linear Concord valve model encased in a mesh grill, through which any drinks could be spilt with devastating outcomes. The Kasbah also broke a record in those early days, for selling the most Coca Cola in the South of England, being the staple drink in between the coffees dispensed by the usual Italian Gaggia machine. On that same corner above the coffee bar stood Avenue Car Sales, run by two successful young businessmen Pete Bailey and Pat Buckle. They were quite taken with our outfit, offering to manage us, with the bonus of their up-market connections, leading to better paid bookings all over the place. A memorable venue that we fondly remember was the Waterfront Club, in the annexe to the Cliff Hotel on Portsmouth Road, Woolston. This was next to the bus station and nearby Floating Bridge Ferry terminal on the banks of the River Itchen, so ideally located. Like the Concorde Club, the Waterfront mainly booked R&B bands from the area as well as

52

visiting groups from London, one of which caused some trouble, as we found out when turning up to play. Owned by Ron Pope, whose son Roger later found fame as drummer for Rod Stewart, Elton John and many more international recording stars, this was always a great venue. It was a long narrow room with the small stage on the left as you walked in, with our heads just under the low ceiling tiles as we rocked the joint on several occasions.

We noticed the damaged panels above us, with the owner complaining about the London-based band that had performed a few nights before. They had packed the place out, with a very loud hard-hitting sound and stage antics including the aggressive lead guitarist bashing out some of the panels. Ron exclaimed *"Those Cockney bastards won't be back here again!"* However, due to public demand that packed the room out, they did return for a couple more appearances until a change of name plus hit records took them onto the world stage. I managed to find this rare advert that probably confirms that you may have already guessed the name of this very band, later demolishing their drums, amps, hotel rooms all over the place!

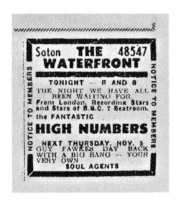

The High Numbers - The Who!

Messrs Bailey and Buckle had several interests across the New Forest, managing to book us into classy hotels and clubs. The 'toffs' seemed to enjoy this long haired bunch of R&B musicians in amongst the more sedate dance bands that were usually playing at these kinds of functions – many of whom tended to look down their stuffy noses at us! We soon got the Hooray Henries and Henriettas jiving away in their tuxedos and ball-gowns, whipping the crowd up with Rolling Stones hits and much more. They certainly let their own hair down on some of these nights as the wine and champagne flowed freely into the small hours. On one occasion I remember us all getting changed into our stage-wear at some posh Hunt Ball, having to pass through the games room, only to avert our eyes from a couple sprawled across the snooker table, engaging in a different kind of 'sport' (potting the pink).

One of the finest Forest venues was the Bure Country Club at Mudeford, booking many big names from the charts, including hit-maker Eden Kane and the Downbeats, featuring his two brothers, later to go on to achieve their own taste of solo fame. We were excited to get booked as the support act, enjoying the taste of the big time by working with a big star, although Eden's recording career was fading away at that time. Kane and his group were amazing, with great harmonies and stage presence that all helped us a little as we watched, learning a bit more. Clive had a minor hit in 1976 with the old Hoagy Carmichael composition of 'My Resistance Is Low' under the name of Robin Sarstedt. Brother Peter had the much bigger hit with his classic haunting release of 'Where Do You Go To My lovely' in 1969, one of the most loved songs of the decade.

I saw Eden Kane again on a recent touring Marty Wilde show in Birmingham. Still looking and sounding as good as ever, after moving to the USA, where he has been kept busy with recording, film and television work. He also travels back to the UK for odd tours with some of the big names of the Sixties.

Itchen Grammar School classmates
(Hoisted by my own petard)
Photo courtesy: Judy Challen – far right

My school studies had suffered during 1964, with the natural distractions of my new path in life, my mind being elsewhere when sitting in the classroom at Itchen Grammar School. My pals at other schools had planned to leave for employment out in the wide world, as there was a lot of it in those boom years, giving them money to spend on records, clothes, scooters and all that went with the freedom to what they wanted. I often fell asleep at my desk, following a late night gig with lack of sleep, with a well-aimed piece of chalk hitting my head to jolt me back to the lesson in hand. It came as no major surprise when my parents received a letter from the headmaster to the effect that it wasn't worth me returning for the autumn term in September. It was not an 'expulsion' as such, as my folks were always supportive of whatever I wanted to do with my life - they could have appealed at the decision but let it go. If I had stayed on for sixth form, followed by university then what the hell was I going to do for the rest of my days? Money was tight, so I didn't wish to burden my parents with the costs of supporting me. As if any 15/16 year old kid really knows what they want to do at that age?

All things American appealed to me from an early age, especially the music, the big flashy cars, comics and a lot more. Tenpin Bowling took off around this time as another US import entered the UK, with new centres springing up all over the country. New purpose-built alleys were constructed, as well as former cinemas being converted, with television coverage of big matches boosting this great new leisure facility. Southampton's first outlet in 1962 was the Top Rank Bowl on Banister Road, next to the old Ice Rink – later taken over by the same company. Across the road being Charlie Knott's Sports Stadium, which staged greyhound racing, followed by speedway and stock car racing. Southampton Speedway ace Barry Briggs was one of the first VIP bowlers on the opening night in August, in full 'Saints' bike leathers, gaining mass press coverage and boosting the profile of this new facility.

During my previous years at the Top Rank Bowl, I had enjoyed being part of the young 'Saints A' team alongside a good pal Tony Brewer. We played in the Saturday morning Junior League, as well as paying visits to other centres around the South, competing against their home teams. Tony's parents Ray and Celia were also keen participants in this newest popular leisure import from the USA, so we kept in touch for many years later. The family first ran a fruit and vegetable shop in Lodge Road, later changing course in setting up a very successful industrial cleaning company, with contracts dealing with local business premises. Going by the name of Bargate Industrial, they soon expanded the client base across the South of England, taking on more staff in the new areas. They were living in a house near the bottom of Chalk Hill, West End, a few doors down from another pal Bob Dunn whose quaint home had an old plaque on the outside wall showing it as 'Thatcher Cottage'. Being a trendy good-looking Sixties type, he quickly painted over four letters to rename it as 'That Cottage' with his bright red Jaguar E-Type parked outside – a real 'Ladies Man' in his youth! Later years saw him hooking up with Barbara Winters, as well as being her manager during their close relationship. Bob was a trained talented chef, later owning his own restaurant in Bevois Valley named 'Peddlers Restaurant' as a nod to one of his favourite modern jazz outfits at the time. We also enjoyed listening to albums by early Chicago, Blood Sweat & Tears, Jose Feliciano plus other contemporary music – played at high volume on his stereo system much to the disdain of the neighbours. After many of my shows at the Woolston pub, we would all pile out to the Bishops Waltham Country Club – a mixed gay/straight venue with a fantastic friendly atmosphere lasting way into the early hours.

My earnings from the Novagraphic photography business were fairly low, with the virtual 'beer money' level wages from the group income hardly making much difference, although still living at home with my parents. To earn some 'pin money' I was offered some temporary late night cleaning work for the Brewers in out of hours offices, cinemas, shops etc as they had all closed for the night. Despite being very well off thanks to Bargate's success, both Ray and Celia Brewer got stuck in with the manual work – real 'hands on' bosses, joining the staff with general cleaning duties, turning up for work in their red Rolls Royce Shadow on occasions! They had acquired the cleaning contract for the chain of the large Top Rank Bingo Halls in London so always needed extra staff in addition to the local workers on the late night shifts. I went along on a few occasions including taking the wheel of Celia's car, being familiar with London streets from an early age by reading maps etc. She was also nervous about driving in the busy capital so this worked out well, plus we never stopped laughing on the way as well as going about the actual work of sweeping up the rubbish, mopping floors etc. I also took the 'scenic route' through the West End, up to Soho, where I pointed out a few famous landmarks as well as mentioning the 'working girls' on the street corners which she had never seen before! One of the bingo halls was the Top Rank Kilburn, a former cinema, to which I would return as a featured entertainer within a couple of years after moving to the capital on my first steps as a solo comedy/vocal/guitar act. Isn't life strange....

The lanes-man at the Top Rank Bowl was a great character by the name of John Heathcote, himself a good bowler who kept the lanes up to professional standards. He also had a beautiful sidekick by the name of 'Whizz', a German Shepherd/Alsatian dog who also kept him company on his overnight shifts when the place was shut for the out of hours maintenance. This also served as a degree of security, as John could quickly command his pet to see off any intruders. One of his wonderful tricks was to move the wooden bowling ball racks along the main concourse, spaced out as an obstacle course, followed by 'Whizz' running and jumping over these 'hurdles' much to the delight of the onlookers. I believe he was also the first local player to achieve the unofficial 'perfect score' of the maximum 300 at the time.

I also got on with the mechanics, being fascinated by the Brunswick pin-setting machines, getting to know how they worked as they kindly allowed me to go 'backstage' to see them in action. The chief mechanic was John Dollery, married to a funny Liverpool lady Joan, who worked in the snack bar, run by a tough smallish guy - Vic Sparrow. If there was any hint of trouble in this area or upstairs in the bar, then Vic was straight in there to sort out any idiots who wanted to start anything. He had a flat nose, so I seem to think that he was a former boxer who may have lost a bout or two? He often floored the odd troublemaker in the snack area or the upstairs bar, before ceremoniously dumping the poor sod outside on the pavement.

The second chief mechanic was Terry Smith, a good-looking 'teddy boy' kind of a teenager, with sleeked back Brylcreemed hair, being the proud owner of a Velocette Venom Clubman 500cc motorbike, with 'fishtail' exhaust pipe. Very powerful machine, which would be worth a small fortune these days, as one of the best ever British bikes and very sought after by vintage collectors. Terry was also very keen on the ladies, some of whom made a discreet entrance through the back door, then into the mechanics' staff room for some fun behind the locked door. I helped him out by sneaking round to the machines, in readiness to fix any breakdowns on the 24 lanes, which were usually simple pin or ball jams. The control desk would send messages over the rear Tannoy system, but knowing that the new 'apprentice' was discreetly covering for the duty mechanic on his 'comfort breaks'. Main guy on the desk was Roger, assisted by another great character Les Davenall who looked after the bowling shoe hire desk. The centre had a busy league schedule throughout the day and night, with many top scoring names achieving record breaking scores. Some of these names still ring a bell, with the likes of Mo Knapp, Clive Thomas, Jon Reeves, Gerry Bugden, and the brilliant Dave Sakkas who achieved international status in the game. Good-looking guy who attracted loads of tenpin 'groupies' whenever he was playing, just like some of our pop groups!

September came along, leading me into my first full-time employment, as I took up an apprenticeship at the Top Rank Bowl on the very same pinsetters. Like many factors in life, I was able to learn stuff fairly quickly, thanks to an inquisitive mind as well as good advice from the chief engineers. We had many laughs in between the work, often playing tricks on unsuspecting bowlers. We could see up the lanes through tiny slits on the large front panels that covered the machines, as well as peering through the lower parts of the assembly. Sitting on a small ledge just above the lane gave us the chance to pick up a solitary pin that was left for a second 'spare' shot just before it reached the spots. Or just knocking more pins over with a thin rod on the first throw. Another giggle was by writing out little notes to any attractive girls, then screwing them up to push into the finger holes of the bowling balls before sending them back along the rack and tunnels. Loved the expressions on their faces as they picked up the ball for their next attempt- unless someone else handled it, risking a jealous boyfriend that we had overlooked!

Lanesman John was later replaced by Ken Radwell, an older more 'serious' kind of guy but nice with it. Overnight closures allowed Ken to carry out his own maintenance in the dark deserted centre, which gave us the opportunity to scare him out of his wits. Three of us had stayed behind, hiding away as the building was locked up at the end of the night's play at ten o'clock. It was quite a spooky place, thus providing us with the chance to play a trick on him. Above the false ceiling panels lay a network of large metal ventilation shafts, solid enough to carry our weight to crawl along to gain access to any part of the upper building structure. One of the mechanics quietly entered the hinged opening panel, stopping just a few feet into the shaft that stretched all along the bowling areas just above where Ken was oiling the lanes as part of the normal maintenance.

I was watching from a dark far corner, as the unsuspecting workman took a cigarette break on the main concourse. This was the cue for my pal to start whispering *"Ken......Ken..."* in a quiet ghostly voice, with the sound enhanced by a natural echo in the shaft. Ken sat bolt upright, looking all around to see where this voice was coming from, swivelling his chair. He was frozen, not daring to move an inch from his seat, until the next prank kicked in as the unseen voice got louder with *"Ken....Ken.... we are coming for you...."* This was the cue for the third prankster who was secreted under the main control desk, then reaching above his head to turn each pinsetter on – one by one, lighting up the machines from the first lane upwards. Ken shot up in a panic, running for the emergency crash door leading to the side of the building, and out into the dark street. We only wish we could have recorded this hilarious stunt, followed by the torrent of bad language and insults from the poor victim who was shaking like a leaf. He cooled down fairly quickly, joining in with the laughter so all ended well.

For some reason, the Abdo-Men were winding down as Dave Sothcott decided to join the Royal Navy, leaving us four remainers to decide what to do next. Another major stroke of fortune came my way, thanks to my good pal Beau, who had been approached by another local group, casting their eye on his vocal talents. This next move resulted in one of my favourite years throughout my blossoming career, although we only earned a few pounds between us with average band fees around the £10-12 mark. Split four or five ways, less fuel and some money for anyone who helped us, along with 10% commission if booked via an agency. We also had to buy our own equipment, so not leaving us with much profit. The money didn't matter - it was fun to rehearse then travel to shows to play for a couple of hours with so many laughs and crazy stunts which we often pulled – as well as the girls! Our teenage years are generally the best times of our lives, so these were no exception as I soaked up the new hit records, trendy clothes and all that went with these times.

Sadly, not many of us have any photographs from our first band days as very few people were using cameras. I was keen on photography but regret not organising any pictures at that time. I only have a 'crap' photo of bass player Geoff Baker 'sitting on his potty' but he doesn't mind me sharing the image! We both still laugh at the crazy antics that we did back in the day, many off and onstage – especially the latter as it makes for a more entertaining show. When any performers are enjoying themselves it carries across to the audiences, making for a good atmosphere. It's all show-business.

Geoff Baker

Just after the Abdos folded, Geoff and Glenn joined forces with singer/songwriter Ken Starks and Colin Allaway to form one of the longest surviving outfits in the area. In recent times, Circle Plantagenet decided to sideline live appearances in favour of spending their time in the recording studio. This has resulted in a series of brilliant CDs, much acclaimed by the music press and critics alike. The albums can be found on the internet with information on their prolific output, or by going to their website.

Whilst completing this book, I was very saddened to hear that Glenn has just passed away early June 2020, having just turned 71. I managed to call him a few weeks before, when learning of his health issues. Good to cheer him up with many more of my mucky gags that kept him laughing. Good pal and talented musician who will be much missed, with a long line of playing with several groups such as the

Rick Brown Band, Circle Plantagenet (then and now), Jelly Roll, Mixed Company, Bob Pearce Blues Band, Rubber Band, The South Coast Pop Art Experimental Band, Streetcar, China Heat plus load of fills in between as a stand-in or 'dep'. These and other local groups will be featured in the follow-up to this first Southern Roots, later on this year.

Circle Plantaganet

Colin   Geoff   Ken   Glenn

https://circleplantagenet.com

Geoff has also racked his brains, having certain memories that I had forgotten about, not helped by my failure to keep a diary of sorts. However, I'm more than happy that old age has not diminished my own recall of people and places from over half a century, relieved to have finally published this book after such a long time. It was started a few years back but sidelined for no apparent reason - better late than never! Geoff writes:

"The beginnings of the Abdos are indeed hazy to me - but as I remember Dave Sothcott and I were in a little band plus a drummer, Richard /Ricky Fagg who was probably 3 or 4 years older than us - significant at that age maybe? I think he was a final year apprentice toolmaker at Fords, possessing a lovely Triumph Bonneville – on which I rode pillion on many times in those days with no helmet requirements - health and safety not around then!! I'm sure he was still just about in the group when we got together?? His dad ran the clothes shop (Leadales?) in St Mary's St opposite Henry's Records as you said - we used to practice in the attic room 3 flights up. I think Richard left because he had a steady girlfriend wanting to focus (or she did....) on the upcoming wedding, followed by getting a 'proper job' when his apprenticeship ended. So then we needed a new drummer.

At some point before he left I believe we had attracted the involvement of a `roadie/would be manager' called Alan (?) who was a bit of a mystery to me - think his parents lived in Peartree Avenue (Woolston end), and I definitely remember Mick Young mimicking his mother "... would you like another cup of tea boys?" I think Alan then said he knew of a drummer (Glenn) to replace Richard - but I'm not totally sure.. Regarding the temporary 'organist' I also seem to remember that somebody drove round late one night to leave the keyboard outside his house with a goodbye note – because of fearing his dad's reaction!

Before moving to Shirley, Dave's mother ran a dry cleaning business in Onslow Rd. I first knew the family when they lived in North East Rd, Sholing and I used to go on the round sometimes in the evenings to collect and deliver the clothes, with various drivers as I was about 14 at the time. One of the houses being Beau's home I am sure. I remember Beau playing a song he wrote - `She's The Girl On My Mind' - does it ring any bells with you - but it didn't get onto our play-list far as I recall.

I recall the Kasbah but didn't realise it was owned by Brian 'Kiwi' Adamson. I remember the manager 'Snowy' Alpine - a rather hard ex Navy man I think. Used to love the Kasbah and of course I lived in the next street so it was my second home for ages. I also remember Pat Buckle, the Bure Club - and a party at Brockenhurst - did we actually play at it or just get invited there? I remember either you or Glenn telling me after the party that they had seen Pat's girlfriend with a love bite at the top of her thigh as she sat legs akimbo in a mini skirt or similar ... got my imagination running as a callow youth I must say....

Didn't we also have a gig at the big Park Hotel in Brockenhurst where the Southampton mayor was in attendance? One of the most memorable gigs I recall was at the Trojans club in Stoneham Lane - which was really rammed, lively and steamy - a combination of us being excellent and the rugby club being full of raucous drunkards I expect! We also did the Banister ballroom and Eastpoint centre - or the school that it was then".

Throughout this book you will be aware that many of my long life friendships have evolved from my years at school, then as a result of striking up new relationships during the group era. Fast forward to 2018, leading to a photograph of three of the original Abdo-Men at Southampton's Concorde Club reunited after 54 years. This was taken at one of the annual 'Back To The Sixties' shows, which I have organised since 2008 featuring many of the top local 60s groups who are still playing or reformed after breaking up way back in their day. Dave Sothcott moved down to Poole, following a spell with the Royal Navy, but has kept up his excellent guitar playing ever since. Beau still busy with Toast, who performed at this 2018 show, giving us a chance to meet up again.

Dave   Beau   David
Concorde Club 2018

The local scene was well established by this time, as many top bands were also inspiring us newer outfits, one of the best being Ricky and the Hi-Lites. They had formed during the early 60s, featuring the superb talents of lead vocalist Rick and Chris 'Burnsy' Brown on lead guitar and vocals. The more unusual angle being that they were the first twin Indian brothers to front a pop group, which also comprised of accomplished Southampton musicians. The Hi-Lites also followed several UK bands travelling across to Germany to play at army bases, as well as the top clubs such as the world-famous Star Club, Hamburg. Rick possessed the greatest soul voice ever, boosted by their whole sound and slick stage moves. This was directly being influenced by the visiting American acts, with choreographed movements as they played the early R&B plus soul music that was gaining popularity.

The town (later elevated to city status in 1964) also boasted the Brook Brothers, whose Everly Brothers style had helped them make the charts with 'Warpaint' and other lesser hits a few years before the group scene exploded. The Soul Agents were another accomplished R&B band, who became Rod Stewart's first backing group around the same time. Likewise, the Meddy Evils, who recorded on the Pye label, also part of the Avenue Artistes' roster of professional groups. The second book in this two-part series ('Southern Roots – Part two) will outline many more of the bands featured on my web-pages across the last few years, plus mentions of solo singers, D.J.s, managers and the dance hall venues that were packed night after night. Much of the information, images and personal memories boosted by the extensive 'Southern Roots' encyclopaedia as already mentioned in this book.

THE UNFORGIVEN 1965

Eastleigh is an outlying suburb of Southampton, ideally situated close to the airport, M27 motorway with major roads leading off to the New Forest to the west, with Portsmouth some twenty miles to the east. The railway works brought prosperity to the area, on the edges of pleasant countryside. The economy was later boosted by the main Ford factory, manufacturing the Transit van which dominated the commercial market for decades. Next to the main Eastleigh rail station, the adjacent car park was built over the site of a much-missed pub, featuring live entertainment for several years. The large function room was always booked for celebrations, meetings and getting very busy with the old dance bands, followed by the new pop groups.

The JunctionHotel Eastleigh

The top band in Eastleigh was formerly known as The Planets, later changing the name to The Unforgiven, being the title of a classic 1960 western, starring Burt Lancaster and Audrey Hepburn. By 1964, the 'Mod' movement was well established, influencing many of the singers and musicians, including lead vocalist John Drever boasting a superb vocal talent plus 'attitude' that suited the current trends. The drummer, Dave Bunney, was lucky enough to have ties with the Junction Hotel, by going out with the licensee's daughter, hence the chance to land the Sunday night residency for the band. Tom Fosberry played bass guitar, later replaced by Steve Newman. A few years ago,

I was pleasantly surprised to receive an e-mail from Tom who, like so many former 60s musicians had discovered my web-pages. He kindly filled in a few more details for which I am grateful - the same goes for everybody else by filling in many gaps or correcting some of the information that I first wrote about. Prior to the Junction gig, the Planets had been rehearsing in the Family Room at the Stoneham Arms on Chestnut Avenue in Eastleigh, plus a residency slot.

They were a slickly organised outfit with printed business cards, thanks to their manager Tony Cook, also having played drums with dance and jazz bands for some years. 'Cookie' as we called him was another major part of my teen years, and a lasting influence on my later career. He was also very kind in allowing me the chance to be part of his precious line-up, albeit by a circuitous route. Tony worked hard as a lorry driver with BRS, later being in charge of a Ready Mix cement mixing truck during the day, before rushing home to drive the Planets all over Hampshire and beyond.

ENTERTAINMENT BEAT GROUP

HAMPSHIRE CHAMPIONSHIP FINALISTS

THE PLANETS

ALL ENTERTAINMENTS CATERED FOR

BIG BEAT and R. & B.

Manager:
J.A. Cook,   Phone:
151 Underwood Road,
Bishopstoke, Eastleigh.

Another special person entered my life, becoming another life long buddy, with an amazing talent that led to bigger things in his long career in the game. Tony was having a drink at the Stoneham Arms, when his ears pricked up at a great sound from the next bar, thinking it was the jukebox belting out the latest Beatles hit record. Upon walking into the next room, he was taken aback to see that it was another bunch of lads who were rehearsing their own new show. The main talent being Eddie Harnett, a lead guitarist with a fantastic vocal range, plus the looks of a pop star that was an all-important bonus in the business. The Planets were in the mood for a change of lead singer, with John Drever wanting to break away into another line-up that suited his style, leading to Eddie being 'poached' from his original group – this happens all the time across the music game. The Abdo-Men had appeared on a show with the Unforgiven, nearing the end of our run so a change was in the air.

'Cookie' was knocked out with Beau's vocal range, making discreet approaches, with an invitation to join his protégés. Beau agreed, but only on one condition that his best buddy (me!) could also be part of the new line-up. This was met with an emphatic refusal, as I was not really needed, due to Eddie being the strong front man, as well as the other members having good voices anyway. I was really surplus to requirements. After some deliberation, Tony and his lads relented, allowing us both to augment what was a great bunch of talent anyway. My added vocals style plus the blues harmonica sealed my fate and good fortune over the next year or so. Our own old Abdo-numbers helped to boost a varied set list with the minimum of rehearsals needed, aided by having four vocalists out front - the harmonies were good too!

Tony Cook

Another change of personnel saw Graham Medley taking over the bass slot, replacing Steve Newman, followed later by a new drummer Ronnie Allen. Both Graham and Ronnie being experienced musicians for a few years prior to being part of the Unforgiven. Graham's first outfit was named The Falcons, with a young Heinz Burt in tow, later part of the chart-topping Tornados of 'Telstar' fame. Heinz later had a short solo career before fading into obscurity, but well remembered by many fans of the 60s scene. We all gelled immediately, becoming good friends for many years to come, with so many laughs on the road and on many stages around the South, mainly booked via Tony Cook's contacts. Better gigs came along as we were also being booked into larger venues via Avenue Artistes, having an impressive stable of top acts. Their own managed bands had the luxury of professional photographs and printed publicity posters, although having slightly more agency commission taken out of their fees to cover these costs, on top of better p.a. equipment. All of my own groups throughout my 60s/70s times were more or less 'indie' bands, without the luxury of better promotion, relying on adults who had connections to any of the musicians. Unfortunately, we rarely took any of our own photographs across my own group years.

Transport was a fun thing, as not all young lads had cars, but relying on relatives to ferry them around, with some even travelling by bus for local shows, then late night lifts home. The Unforgiven had no 'bandwagon', so it was a case of Cookie cramming five of us his into his 1960 Ford Consul 375, with a roof rack, a trailer on the back plus a full boot. Latecomer Ronnie had his own small works van, enabling him to transport his drum kit plus overspill amps that could not fit into the 'Cook-mobile' as we named it. Having day jobs, it was always a mad rush to get home, fed, changed then straight out for the evening ahead. Army bases on Salisbury Plain were a constant source of our shows, plus many top venues all over Hampshire and beyond. The Winchester Lido Ballroom was another major run of successful nights, having hosted many top chart hit-makers such as the Rolling Stones, Hollies etc.

It was also used for the popular all-in wrestling nights, with the fixed bouts, theatrical gimmicks, costumes and the like – all part of show-business! Usually booked through Avenue Artistes, always leading to Len Canham wandering backstage, as he cooked up some of his food for the night on a small stove in the kitchen, which doubled as the groups' changing rooms. His timing was always impeccable, just as each group was getting dressed, dropping our trousers in readiness to wear stage clothes for the performance! 'Auntie' Len, as we called him, was never too predatory as such, so we all just laughed it off as he gazed around the room. They had three stages around the large room, with three different bands set on each one for the evening. Dave Bunney still laughs about the time he was setting up his kit, as Len sidled up behind him, patting him gently on the bum, saying *"Just move your bass drum a little more forward – that's a dear boy..."*

'Bunney-Boy' as we called him reminds me of another eventful night at the Junction Hotel, as yet another punch-up broke out towards the end of an otherwise great evening. It was a common occurrence,

71

started by the usual local suspects, fuelled by booze and just looking for trouble. Often kicked off by someone chatting up the wrong girl, accidentally bumping into someone or by 'outsiders' rolling up from another rival area. Dave writes:

"I remember one Sunday, when playing the Junction, a fight started. There were chairs flying about everywhere with everyone seemingly involved. We stopped playing as they were invading our space. The other lads moved quickly away from the trouble, out into the car park, but I was trapped behind my drum kit in the corner. My only escape route was the nearby window, so hurriedly climbed out backwards, sliding down a drainpipe into the garden area, only to have landlord Alf Shepherd's vicious guard dog bite me on the arse! Then straight back up into the room, waiting for the mini-riot to calm down.

Dave Bunney

Alf's wife kept tropical fish, on show in every room of the Junction, much admired by everyone. Sadly, in the middle of this fight, some idiot was seen to pour a pint of beer into the large tank, which killed all of the beautiful fish. The police arrived to break it all up, sort out who was to blame for starting the trouble but met with a wall of stony silence as was always the case. Alf later apologised on behalf of his dog, but couldn't stop laughing about it all. He was a good guy, letting us rehearse at the pub in between our resident nights. These punch-ups were always an occupational hazard for groups in ballrooms across the country as many will testify, but were generally safe if on a high stage away from the main action. Sometimes, the musicians out front would pick up a heavy microphone stand in readiness, which usually did the trick by deterring anyone who got too close for comfort. Happy days!"

Having reached the grand old age of 16, I was able to buy my first second hand motorbike, choosing a firm favourite of that era – a silver hand-painted 125 cc BSA Bantam. Passed my test shortly after, taking great pleasure in ripping up the L plates in the time-honoured tradition. I soon sold it in order to buy a beautiful black and white 250cc Francis Barnett, with tall handlebars and rear guards – my 'mini Harley Davidson'.

Biker Boy!

We usually travelled in Tony's Consul, although I sometimes went on my motorbike to local gigs. This was still the time of Mods and Rockers but I confused people by wearing Mod clothes whilst riding a bike - I was a 'Mocker'! Never wore 'sensible' protective clothes, or even a crash helmet like most bikers in these days, but I wasn't a speed merchant as such.

Christmas day 1965 saw a few of us invited to Tony and Jean Cook's house, for a great meal, booze with most of the day being spent by a marathon of joke-telling which went on for hours. This mainly between Beau and myself, as we kept bouncing off each other with gag after gag. Tony was taking it all in, mentioning that I should consider being a real comedian when (and if) I eventually 'grew up'! This stuck in my mind, never forgetting his encouragement, although it took another few years before I realised that I needed to make a solo break away from what was then becoming a stagnant music scene in 1972. We had so much fun on the road, having several near-misses as Tony was laughing so much, not concentrating on the road ahead!

I still smile at some of the memories when we were playing at the Stonehenge Inn on Salisbury Plain - a regular group venue, but often ending up with drunken squaddies having punch-ups between themselves or with the local lads who had a go! We just kept on playing as bottles, chairs, tables and soldiers came flying through the air in front of us - luckily they never bothered with the band, but encouraged us to keep going in case the noise attracted anyone outside of the building! I was actually 'spotted' by another group at this function room in the village of Durrington Walls, very close to the old ruins that gave the pub its name. I would return to the area in 1967, for yet another spell with more new pals.

Beau played a good rhythm guitar, apart from having one of the best voices around (still does!) but being a little shy in those early days. Both of us had to learn many new songs, as we slotted into this new group, although I only had my blues harmonica that was easy to busk, such is the ad-lib nature of the instrument. Beau was not too sure about some of the more complex chord structures and arrangements of certain numbers. This soon became apparent when we noticed that he seemed to discreetly lower his volume control knob at odd times. As soon as Ed launched into a solo break, we could only hear the bass guitarist and drummer playing along, as the sound diminished. On the next gig, the rest of us had a private chat about it, deciding to play a game to catch him out. We kicked off the show, before settling on a particularly difficult tune that we knew was a problem with Beau. Half-way through the number, I was keeping an eye on his hands then gave a pre-arranged signal for everyone to stop dead. Beau was smiling away, strumming his guitar but no sound coming out of the amp, which resulted in a hasty knob-twiddle to crank it up again, but too late. We all collapsed into a giggling heap, with a confused floor of dancers who stopped in their tracks, wondering what the hell we were playing at. Beau's embarrassment soon turned to him laughing along with us, with a few expletives that were luckily not picked up by the microphone! It didn't take him much longer to learn every new number chord by chord, so all ended well. A couple of years later, he switched to bass guitar - quite a challenge when singing different notes to the actual bass line being played. His superb talents have seen him play with several top bands to this day, the latest being 'Toast' with a massive following all over the Hampshire area. In addition, he was also part of 'Brownhills Stamp Duty' fronted by Rick Brown, of previous 'Hi-Lites' fame as you will have read about. More of this in the next book in the series.

Another hilarious time at the Stonehenge Inn near Amesbury being when we finished playing, then packing the gear up along with chatting up the local girls, although watching out for jealous boyfriends hanging around the door. We sometimes needed the bouncers to escort us out of the pub car park on several occasions as well as keeping an eye out on return shows. A heavy summer storm was lashing down, as Tony backed the Consul and trailer up to the front door, in readiness for the equipment to be carried out. We were still on the pull inside, mingling with the girls as per usual after any show, having no idea that the poor guy was soaking wet, standing on the trailer, drenched to the bone. We immediately stopped when hearing a barrage of expletives being shouted by the entrance door, then realising that it was a livid Cookie. *"Come on you f*****g bunch of lazy bastards – get the damned gear out here NOW!"* We fell about laughing as he got angrier and angrier, threatening to drive off and leave us all there. The equipment was quickly loaded into the car, followed by five hot sweaty wet musicians, causing the windows to steam up with the condensation, with Cookie still 'steaming', his blood pressure hitting the roof. It was made worse as we could not stifle our laughter, but he soon cooled down as we hit the road. It was all forgotten as we cracked gags, plus singing a few songs back to Eastleigh. Tony's wife Jean was an angel, often treating us to tea, toast and biscuits whenever we rolled up in the middle of the night, as well as making some sandwiches before leaving for any show a few hours before. Tony and Jean also looked after Eddie, whose family had split up by then, taking him into their guardianship with a permanent room at their home. He became one of the family, alongside the young Clive and Lesley Cook who then had a new 'big brother' to look up to, later joined by a new young sister Rachel, all of whom remaining my great friends for many years to come.

Former bass player, Tom Fosberry, also mentioned another episode: *"I remember the Consul and trailer. If Cookie was tired, I used to drive it for him. I didn't pass my test until some four years later. One particular gig remains in my memory, and that was at Bulford Camp Sergeants Mess. Cookie being Cookie had forgotten to fuel up the Consul, and as a result we ran out of petrol on the top of Pepperbox Hill near Salisbury. Dave Bunney and I walked to Romsey railway station, managing to hitch a ride on the milk train and got back to Eastleigh around four in the morning."*

Jean and Tony Cook

Group vans and cars were always breaking down, as most were older vehicles, but sometimes turning out well. Another incident still reminds me of the time when the Unforgiven were booked into a major ballroom up in Surrey, via Avenue Artistes who dealt with other offices around the South. Woking Atlanta Ballroom was a massive dance hall, run by the Bob Potter Agency. Bob had previously owned a scrap-yard, before moving into managing the new pop groups in the late Fifties, himself being a musician with several dance bands in that part of the country. Some years later, he opened the Lakeside Country Club in Frimley Green, becoming one of the top nightspots in the UK. This prestigious venue has seen a host of top names perform there, as well as hosting several world champion darts matches, being televised as many will know.

We had left Southampton, travelling up the old main A33 road towards London, merging into the A30 as the M3 motorway was not built until the Seventies. A few miles out, the Consul juddered to a halt, with steam escaping from under the bonnet, so lucky to make it to a lay-by. We all got out of the car to see what could be done, but the clock was ticking, causing a great deal of worry. There was an AA box close by but Cookie was not a member at that time, so we were all panicking. Just then, a massive American car glided in behind us, the driver needing to stop to stretch his legs. He was bemused to see us all standing by the trailer full of our musical equipment, enquiring to see if any help was needed. He was intrigued with our plight, kindly offering to take the band members, with the guitars that fitted into the massive boot, up to Woking which was not too far from where he actually lived. This was a great stroke of luck, especially for me, loving the classic 50/60s 'Yank Tanks' as they were known. Heads were turned by the young fans queuing outside of the dance hall, waiting for the doors to open, as this beautiful gold-coloured Pontiac Parisienne rolled up into the car park. As soon as we got out, picked up the guitars and stage clothes, I guess they all thought that some bigger name group was making a surprise guest appearance on the show? Sad to disappoint them, but we had a successful night, borrowing the other band's amps, drums and p.a. equipment. Poor Cookie had managed to get some help with the car, then limping slowly back to Eastleigh to wait up for us to get back in the early hours.

There were other times when noticing that something had fallen off the trailer as we drove along some road, due to not being tied down properly. When at the wheel, Tony always kept looking in the rear mirror, so any falling object was noticed before any following traffic could crush it! Slammed on the brakes - jumped out, swearing like a trooper, having to tie it all up again as we sat in stitches inside the car! It was usually one of the hard drum cases that were always placed on top, so strong enough to survive any ejection onto the road! He always settled down quickly, then joining in with the merriment, having a terrific sense of humour, coming out with some funny lines and sayings himself. Self-deprecating about his big stick-out ears, as we all took the mickey out of these appendages – he often responded to our conversations by cupping his hands to the side of head, saying *"Go on – tell me- I'm all ears!"* He also roared when I compared his head to a taxi with two doors open and other one-liners. Looking back, we did give him a bit of a hard time, but we all appreciated how much work and effort he put into running the Unforgiven. It was his – and our passion, so there were never any big fall-outs as were too busy enjoying the ride. Wonderful man.

Beau remembers an even worse, but another hilarious occasion, when we were all returning from a gig in Salisbury, arriving in Southampton city centre, heading for the best late night food outlet for hungry musicians. Mike's Burger van had the prime location in a lay-by opposite the Police Station, part of the Civic Centre, being very convenient for the coppers on their own late night shifts across the road. This spot was just by the old Marlands Hall ballroom, another well-known dance venue, the site now occupied by the BBC Radio Solent complex. Most travelling bands stopped here in the early hours, chatting to each other as we compared notes on how our shows went.

The Consul needed petrol as we headed along Millbrook Road leading into town, with the handy Tilbury's garage and its twenty four hour operation being one of these rare overnight fuelling locations, opposite the main railway station. Cookie slowed down, turning right onto the forecourt with a very tight turning circle needed. This put a strain on the over-loaded trailer, leading to a loud cracking noise as the metal linking assembly gave way, resulting in the trailer coming adrift in the middle of the road. Once again, Lady Luck was on our side, thanks to little traffic being on the road at that late hour. We all jumped quickly out to retrieve the stricken wagon before our instruments were written off by a passing car or lorry. The garage attendant was kind enough to let us offload the broken trailer, to leave the gear in the office for a couple of hours as we had to be dropped off home. It was then a case of waking parents up in order to drive to Tilburys to retrieve the equipment, with Cookie having to patch up the broken linking gear, followed by a slow cautious journey back home.

THE UNFORGIVEN – ON TOUR!

Many Southerners head for the West Country on summer breaks, incurring a long hard drive along A-roads, then onto other routes to get to the coastal resorts. The Cook family had booked a caravan in Polzeath on the north Cornish coast, as well as inviting Eddie, Dave Bunney and my good self to join them by bringing a couple of small tents. Not the best location on top of a small hill, which caused a problem as Eddie and Dave set up their own tent, with me next to them in my own. On the first early morning, a storm blew in, with heavy rain and strong winds, resulting in my canopy blowing away. The other lads had looked out, seen this happen but just laughed as I was still snoring away in my sleeping bag, not aware of the sudden loss of the roof!

Polzeath Beach

1965 also witnessed the new West Coast music that was gradually being imported from the USA, as the 'Hippie' culture was growing fast. Bob Dylan had provided the Byrds with a UK chart-topper with 'Mr Tambourine Man', followed up with a British tour that same summer. Eddie had a passing resemblance to David Crosby, leading to some girls on the nearby beach taking notice as we were all kicking a ball around the beach. They had naturally thought that this chart-topping band were in the area, so made a bee-line for Ed, calling out *"David - David!"* They had obviously heard one of our group calling out for *"David!"* to pass the ball, as there were two of us, so misleading them further. Ed twigged this immediately, as we had just been talking about this great record plus including it in our up to date set-list. So - he broke into a run, as the fans chased him for a few hundred yards until the reality sunk in, leading to more fun with the young ladies. It really was non-stop merriment all the way, leaving us with so many wonderful memories to cherish for the rest of our lives.

Eddie   David

Certain place names stick in the mind, usually the odd ones. One of these amused us greatly being a small village that we passed through on this trip, with the wonderful name of Pendoggett, a few miles from our beach location. I asked Tony to stop the car on the main road, winding down the car window to ask a local for some directions to Polzeath. This was all in French, having done fairly well with my school studies, so giving the impression that we were a carload of foreign tourists. Confusion reigned for a few minutes as the poor unsuspecting villager tried his best to explain with arm motions, directions plus slow drawn-out speech as one does when faced with this problem. I then thanked him, in perfect Queens English *"Thank you very much – you've been most kind old chap. Goodbye"!"* We then drove off slowly, looking back at the bemused pedestrian, scratching his head in bewilderment.

Another one of my stunts was pretending that my hand was stuck in the slot of a post box, as I had *"accidentally posted a letter but forgot to stamp it"*. Polzeath village was the usual stage for this bit of harmless fun, thronged with holidaymakers who stopped in their tracks at my 'predicament'. Concerned passers-by gathered round to offer advice as our lot stood close by, suppressing their mirth. One time, a nearby shopkeeper came out with a bowl of soapy water, in case this might help to free my hand, but managing it myself. If only we had camera-phones back then! This photo shows me pulling the same trick back home in Woolston, thus giving you the basic idea. If anyone reading this was taken in all those years ago – I hope   I'm 'forgiven'....

Return to Sender?

Christmas 1965 was a busy month for us all, with one of our repeat visits to Clarence Pier Ballroom next to the beach at Southsea, entertaining the friendly Portsmouth audiences, despite hailing from a 'rival' town! Upon leaving the stage with our equipment, we had to walk through the deserted kitchens, used for the general catering of the entertainment complex. This led out to a back alley, being the main loading area for service vehicles and visiting acts. One of us noticed massive unlocked chest freezers, leading to the lifting of lids to see what lay within. Allegedly - for some reason, empty drum cases were utilised to serve as temporary storage for a few frozen turkeys, destined for tables on the next festive function. These apparently ended up on plates some twenty odd miles back in Southampton, with no food poisoning being reported as a result of de-frosted meat after a couple of hours on the road. I trust that the Statute of Limitation would not be implemented some 65 years later? This is the official ruling in the UK:

"The purpose of having a statute of limitation is to prevent charges from being raised that date so far back into the past that defence against the charges is difficult and expensive. Evidence might be difficult to obtain, testimony may be clouded, and the defendant/s may not receive a fair trial".

Dave Bunney has his own memory of that festive frolic, his mother waking him up on the Sunday morning to inform him that some water was dripping out of a drum case in the hall. Lo and behold, two large defrosting birds had been placed there, following the Southsea gig but without his knowledge. Dave firmly suspected our bass player who denied it all, but not preventing the Bunney household from enjoying their Christmas bonus that year. We always joked that they only had rabbit everyday. Quite often, a last-minute show would come in for any band, for a variety of reasons. Usually the case of filling in for another group who could not make their booking, or sometimes due to overlooking the diary page.

Dave was a keen cinema patron, often to be found at the local Eastleigh picture house with his latest current girlfriend. The first interruption came after about ten minutes from the start, when Tony had entered the auditorium after bluffing his way past the staff, due to *"a family emergency"*. The couple always sat in the back row, for the usual obvious reasons but their canoodling was suddenly interrupted by a loud whisper from the aisle. *"Dave Bunney...Dave Bunney.."* It was one of those late fills, with the car, trailer and the lads parked at the front, so it was a quick goodbye to the girl left on her own, not helped by the embarrassment as nearby people were annoyed by the interruption, plus having to stand up as Dave had to make his way stumbling along the aisle out of his seat. This happened two more times, leading to his being dumped by the poor lady whose patience had been truly tested.

Our main achievement came that same year, by entering the group into 'The Battle of the Bands' competition. This was an annual event, part of the Eastleigh Carnival Week, held at the Town Hall in which local pop groups tried to impress the judges. Our main rivals were a new 'Mod' group led by John Drever, the stakes being pretty high as we had to try and upstage them. We stormed the audience with a tight set, dressed in smart blue jackets and ties, with white trousers, enhanced by a few stage antics that grabbed the judging panel of local bigwigs. I cannot remember how much we won as the outright winners - hardly life-changing sums of money, but elevating our profile. This led to more bookings, pushed by an article in the Southern Evening Echo along with this photo below.

THE UNFORGIVEN

Back Row: L-R Eddie, Graham, Dave
Front: Beau, David

There were so many wonderful places to play in these 'boom' years, including 'Room at the Top', formerly known as the Imperial Ballroom on Market Street in Eastleigh town centre. Like many of these dance halls across the country, it was situated on top of Burtons the Tailor, the only problem being the access up a steep staircase adjacent to the shop front. This was a major headache when groups had to lug their equipment up and down the concrete steps, but worth it for a great night out. The club was run by local entrepreneur John Ferris, who booked local and 'name' acts from the London area. The Unforgiven were lucky on one of the big shows, being booked as the support act to the Paramounts from Southend. They had made the charts in 1964 with a superb cover of 'Poison Ivy', the old Coasters hit, that many of used in our own act. Their brilliant lead guitarist, Robin Trower, along with keyboard player Gary Brooker, later shuffled the band around, resulting in a name change to Procol Harum.

We all often do things on a whim, one of mine being influenced by a quirky 1965 British film called 'The Knack (and how to get it)' starring Ray Brooks as a 'Ladies Man' mentoring a shy young Michael Crawford in the art of chatting up the girls, including Rita Tushingham. Brooks played the part of cocky musician Tolen, who rode a motorbike, which immediately struck a chord with me! It was all based on the 'Swinging London' atmosphere that was building at that time.

Shortly after its release, I was reading a copy of Melody Maker, glancing through the classified adverts at the back of the music paper. A new group by the name of 'The Knack' were looking for a lead vocalist, so I thought this was a 'sign' telling me to apply. The major problem being that they were based in Great Yarmouth, some 232 miles away with over four hours travelling time. They had apparently been approached by a record company, so I thought that this might a chance for me to 'make it' as do all aspiring pop stars!

I didn't really want to leave Southampton at that age, but casually mentioned it to my uncle Arthur next door. He laughed and said *"Let's do it – let's have a day out!"* I phoned the Knack's manager who was most surprised at my willingness to make this long journey, in order to audition for the group. We set off very early, in his Ford Anglia driving up the country and across to the Norfolk coast, with the lack of any decent motorways at that period. I did the audition, clicked with the group and their style of music which was more or less what I was into, but I didn't feel confident enough to uproot from my home comforts to take a trip into the unknown.

The group never made it big, so maybe just as well and back to reality with another local group. Arthur had always been there for me, from my very early inroads to the music scene, for which I am eternally grateful. He was a very special person, but cruelly taken away by the awful pandemic that swept in unannounced during March 2020. This is why I have dedicated this book to his memory. R.I.P.

CHUCK BERRY

Most musicians and songwriters will admit to being heavily influenced by this incredible character whose lyrics beamed out the images of teenage years in the American Fifties, weaving stories of cars, railroads, drive-in movies and much more. Adding these songs to a driving R&B guitar-based shuffle beat just took us all to a different dimension as most of us featured many of these songs, during the early Sixties. I just worshipped the Beatles and Rolling Stones - both of whom owe a great debt to Chuck Berry as their early set lists show. In fact - the first Stones UK single was a cover of "Come On" back in July 1963 which kick-started the British R&B boom, helping to refresh the careers of many old Blues performers. I adored the Stones driving beat, plus suddenly discovering a new note-bending talent on blues harmonica which I still play these days when sitting in with a band and jamming away!

The Gaumont Cinema Theatre was the main local venue that hosted many of the top names on 'package tours'. For a few shillings - you could watch the big stars on the same bill, although they only performed for around 15-30 minutes each, depending on their stature. Cliff Richard and the Shadows were one of my earliest memories, later adding more to my list of concerts. To see the likes of Jerry Lee Lewis, Little Richard, Everly Brothers, then the Beatles and Stones was just amazing, especially as these favourite artistes were in their prime.

Thanks to this new 'beat' boom, Chuck Berry had been re-discovered, then toured the country with a superb set of supporting artistes. My precious ticket was for the second house on January 16th 1965. This package show was heavily R&B influenced with the first half featuring the Five Dimensions, Winston G, The Graham Bond Organisation with Long John Baldry closing the first half before the interval. The curtains opened for the main attraction, with a warm-up spot by the fantastic Moody Blues whose first single "Go Now" had just hit the no. 1 spot in the UK charts. The comedian/compere then had to entertain the impatient audience, who were calling out *"Chuck-Chuck-Chuck"* non-stop, with a few warm-up gimmicks in the time-honoured tradition. This short fill was needed as the stage was re-set in readiness for the much awaited top of the bill act.

At last - the curtains opened as the Five Dimensions belted out that familiar rhythm with Chuck Berry strutting onto a thunderous ovation, proceeding to play so many classic songs along with his terrific stage presence. His cheeky facial expressions plus innuendo-laden lyrics were enhanced by his guitar playing with showmanship to the fore. He looked and moved so cool, shuffling around the whole stage, lifting the roof as he slid into the famous 'Duck Walk' then scooting across the front. He was known to be very frugal, following years of being ripped off by unscrupulous US managements, like many of his contemporaries. This saw Chuck demand the full cash payment in advance on the night, failing which he would simply walk out. He was also careful not to pay out for his own backing musicians when on tour, not forgetting a major expense in flying a US band over, with wages, hotels and other travel expenses. The Musicians Union rules also prevented overseas groups from working in the UK, unless reciprocal arrangements were made to allow British artistes to perform in the USA.

Whenever guest acts were touring the UK, the tour companies had a regular list of top backing musicians who were able to accompany any of the big names. Some of the headlining acts had professional music arrangements, known as 'dots', whilst others depended on the high calibre of the home-grown instrumentalists to do their best if merely 'busking'. Fortunately, most of Chuck Berry's set list comprised his well known hits, making it relatively easy for Sounds Inc. on this tour. However, they had no idea what was coming next as Chuck just did his own thing, to quote the 60s saying. They only knew his opening number, followed by a case of picking up the key and riff churned out by the 'master' out front, so very much ad-libbing it all.

It was one of the best shows I have ever seen, but ending far too soon as the curtains closed with the National Anthem ("God Save the Queen") being played as was the protocol at that time! Most people just stood courteously still, waiting for the music to end before leaving the auditorium - can you imagine that these days?? It also gave the stars a chance to dash off-stage, then straight into the waiting cars or disguised vans to whisk them out of the way before they got trapped by fans who were screaming at the sight of their idols just a few feet away. Security wasn't that well organised back then, with many stars feeling frightened as hysterical fans climbed all over the cars in an effort to talk to them, or grab an autograph plus ripping off bits of clothes and even souvenir hair if possible! The Beatles were the main targets of the time, either being trapped in the theatre for hours, or being smuggled out in decoy vehicles, police vans and the like.

I was close to the emergency exit leading to the stage door in a narrow alleyway running down the side of the building, so I quickly sneaked out, clutching my tour programme in case I might be lucky enough to catch a glimpse of the man himself. The waiting Ford Consul had its engine running, so I knew Chuck was on the way out. I was on the opposite side of the car, by the rear passenger door, looking over the roof where several policemen had formed a human barrier to keep the growing number of fans at a distance.

The doors flew open as a hot sweaty Chuck came dashing out of the building, straight into the car, which was facing up the side alleyway. I immediately noticed that the doors were not locked as the plunger was sticking up (no central locking as in modern vehicles) so impulsively grabbed the handle to find that I could open the door. Without a thought, I jumped in to land right next to the man himself, as the car started to move slowly up the hill, trying to avoid the screaming fans that were blocking the way. Amidst this chaotic scramble, the frustrated driver hadn't noticed the extra passenger on the back seat for the first few seconds. His angry response was *"Get that f*****g kid outta here!"* but Chuck just laughed it all off, saying with his wonderful slow Southern Missouri drawl *"No Man......just give the boy a ride - let's keep moving."* I was talking ten to the dozen, saying how much I loved his music, reeling off a list of the songs that us young Brit bands were using. He smiled, saying *"Why son – you know more about my music than I do!"*

The car finally made it to the top of the ramp, with the police keeping everybody away as we turned left onto Commercial Road, down the hill to turn right into Morris Road leading up to the Polygon area of the town, where we pulled over. He kindly signed my programme (pictured) This remains a crystal clear memory, still fresh in my mind after some fifty five years. He signed my programme saying *"Now you go home and be a good boy now!"* I met him again a couple of years later after another show, having discovered he was staying at a hotel off the Avenue. I strolled in, had another chat as he was sitting in the reception with a late night drink, but then quickly ushered out by the desk clerk.

He had remembered me straight away, as the cheeky lad that jumped into the car before. Again, we talked about his music, finding him to be one of the nicest stars I have ever met, despite some stories that he could be 'difficult' on some occasions. I also recall a well-documented story when the Stones knocked on his dressing room door, but were told to come back later as Chuck was 'too busy' to meet them! The story goes that they meekly wandered off muttering *"Hmmph - we ain't gonna do any of his f*****g songs again!"* That was certainly 'No Particular Place To Go'

I still have that programme after all these years, often thinking back to that night when I met one of the greatest legends, whose music and talent have inspired generations of young musicians to this day.

My official signed programme

THE EARTH ANGELS 1966

The next phase of my Sixties journey was a short spell with a new 'trendy' group, encompassing the 'Mod' profile of covering obscure R&B tracks from imported 45s, mixed with Who, Small Faces, plus the usual standard set-list that most of us teen outfits tended to replicate.

I replaced former lead vocalist/harmonica player Melvyn Day, who moved onto other groups for a few years, before relocating to Sheffield. Another of my good musician pals, Bob Pearce, was managing the Earth Angels - the name taken from a 1954 Penguins hit, the American group being in the popular 'Doo-Wop' fashion of the time. Bob knew that I could slot into Mel's shoes, leading to more great times with new mates. Ernie Fagg (bass), Barry Morrow (gtr) Derek Edmonds (Drms) Roy Cooper (gtr) who was then replaced by Melvyn McRae, who passed away a few years ago. I'm always glad to keep in touch with any of my former pals, including Mel Day, meeting up with him a short while ago, when passing through Sheffield. He is still in the game, with his own superb blues band, along with jamming with other musicians, as we all do in our old age! Drummer Derek Edmond has recently moved back to Southampton, after many years in Milton Keynes, where he played with groups as well as giving drum lessons to all ages. It was also good to work with him on a recent Sixties Theme Show at Southampton's Concorde Club, as I have organised an annual event there since 2008 - more of that story later.

Bob Pearce is also one of Southampton's revered musos, carving out a long recording career with solo and groups over the decades. We both started around the same time in 1964, as he formed his first blues band, by the name of The Footprints - another lead vocal, harmonica man, so we are 'kindred spirits'. Again, I have many memory gaps in past years, not able to recall much of what the Earth Angels did, but it was an enjoyable time yet again. We did appear in the ballroom at a unique landmark building constructed in 1935, close to the beach at Lee On Solent a few miles along the coast towards Gosport. This was a small, but popular resort throughout the summer months, being another younger childhood memory as our family enjoyed day trips by the sea.

The Tower Cinema was on the left of the main edifice, boasting a 120 foot tower rising up from the middle, as this old image shows.

Lee Tower 1950s (source unknown)

These bookings came about as a result of my new job as the service engineer downstairs in the small ten lane bowling alley. The former cinema had closed in 1958, adapting to a bingo club plus staging all-in wrestling nights, both being very much in vogue in the early Sixties. Tenpin bowling was another growing leisure activity around the same time, leading to Buccaneer Bowling Ltd taking out the lease on the building in 1964.

The layout of the old cinema walls forced an unusual planning headache, with the outer lanes of 1 & 2 and 9 & 10 being set back from the middle six lanes. This was rather distracting for bowlers getting ready on their approach area on lanes 3 and 8, as the adjacent heavy balls were dropped right next them before rolling noisily down the lanes! The centre was owned by an elderly gentleman, Mr Schumaker, with his main manager running the place, by the name of Joe – a slightly eccentric ex-officer with the Royal Navy, which as always had a large presence in the surrounding Portsmouth area. Joe was a very well-spoken funny guy, often criticising some of the more uncouth types that graced the alley. His label of calling them *"pesky peasants!"* still resonates after all this time, as I can still picture him and laugh. I only worked the day shift, entirely due to my motorbike's lights not working properly, which would been hazardous if riding back through the dark country lanes back to Woolston, some thirteen miles away! Joe's assistant became another new friend of mine, a young Tony Valente, hailing from nearby Gosport, being part of the well-known Italian family of ice cream shop fame in the town. We clicked right away, as he took control of the main reception area plus looking after the pin-setting machines in my absence, with a basic knowledge of how they worked.

The Earth Angels (less me)

My Earth Angels' days ran their course, as I was looking towards a more commercial kind of music, heavily influenced by the 'Flower Power' movement ushered in by the West Coast hippies. I left the band on good terms, as well handing in my notice at the Lee Tower Bowl, with a better new job being offered. You will have probably read about my younger passion for all things American, as their influences were shaping the UK culture with the music, movies, tenpin bowling, cars and that all-important jukebox that helped to trigger my first journey onto a stage. Apart from the aforementioned Kasbah Coffee Bar on London Road, the other best place for us teens was the Checkpoint Café, situated in a small alleyway to the east side of the Bargate. We all passed many an hour sipping coffee or Coca Cola, listening to the latest hits on the jukebox or spending our hard-earned pocket money on feeding it. The lucky older ones had jobs so able to spend more than others, with the bonus of visiting merchant seamen who had money to burn, after long lucrative sailings.

This popular hook-up spot was owned by Reg and Leigh Bicknell, who also ran the nearby Adam & Eve nightclub on Spa Road, to the rear of the old Echo newspaper office block. The area was cleared some years ago, with the new West Quay shopping centre being built on the same site. This small club sported one of the best disco nights in the South, with several local disc-jockeys spinning the vinyl on the twin turntables. The music was bang up to date, with the emphasis on R&B, Soul and Tamla Motown hits that kept them dancing all night. Female DJs were very rare at that time, but a new resident blonde girl soon attracted the club-goers, in the beautiful shape of Carole Hamilton. She still lives in the area, providing her own retro 'Adam & Eve Reunion Nights', playing the same records from those early times, bringing in a wide age range of old - and new fans. The club also booked local and national groups, thus providing a classy live music venue.

The Bicknells later divorced on amicable terms, still running these two places together. Reg was another well-known character, a former racing driver, who had built his own cars with some success in the Fifties at Brands Hatch and other top courses. Having retired from the sport, he set up a used car sales in Hill Lane, just a few yards up from the junction with Commercial Road, close to the main railway station. Apart from the usual mix of second hand cars, Revis Car Sales was also one of the first Skoda dealers in the country, importing these low cost vehicles from Czechoslovakia, as it was then known. We all know that this make of cheap car ended up as the butt of many jokes in the years that followed, but they were not that bad as I recall. In recent times, Skoda has had a major turnaround, rating highly across the motoring world, with reasonably priced models that sell in high figures.

Reg was a great businessman, always smartly-dressed, with the gift of the gab as befits a racing driver, plus the good looks that charmed many a lady in his prime. His hair had turned a lovely grey colour, leading to friends labelling him as the 'Silver Fox', which he didn't mind at all. Guess you could say that he was a bit of a playboy throughout the Sixties and Seventies. He was aware that jukeboxes were great money spinners, as the cash kept rolling in throughout the day, especially at the Checkpoint. These machines were generally installed on a rental basis by local firms, the main supplier being Liberty Coin at the bottom of St Mary's Street, opposite the Central Hall. This successful business had been founded by American Herbie Katz who had settled in the area during the Fifties. He was a main importer of jukeboxes, pintables and fruit machines, which he either sold on or placed them into coffee bars, pubs and clubs on a rental basis.

This successful kind of business prompted Reg to open up his own company, with a small workshop at the back of the main office premises with adjacent car showroom on the corner down from his sales area. I'm not sure how I came to work for him, as a young assistant service engineer to Colin Brown, the main mechanic, who soon taught me how to fix and maintain these wonderful machines all over Hampshire. We skived quite a lot, as there were no such things as mobile phones in those days, so no chance of the office knowing exactly where we were! Our daily duties comprised of servicing the machines in the workshop or travelling from place to place to fix any problems that the owner had reported by phoning in. Plenty of time to stop for a few tea breaks or do any shopping that was needed. Revis had managed to secure several naval shore bases around the Portsmouth area, installing pintables in the NAAFI locations plus fruit machines in the officers' messes, these having large takes as they were very well paid with low outgoings as part of the Armed Forces.

Our main service vehicle was a two-seater Morris Minor van, with enough space to transport amusement machines in the back. I only had my motorbike licence when starting at Revis, but this did not stop me from taking the wheel whenever we drove to remote country lanes. The best opportunity being in the remote Meon Valley, near Petersfield on the South Downs, as the small lanes led through a beautiful wooded forest known as 'Little Switzerland'. HMS Mercury was one of many Navy shore bases tucked away on top of a hill, providing me with the chance to negotiate tight bends and blind corners, without the worry of being stopped by the police. My driving was pretty good, but there was one occasion when my new skills let me down, as this (staged) photograph shows. We had to get help as the wheels were stuck in the mud!

Our favourite visit was always heading for HMS Collingwood, near Gosport, one of the largest shore bases, mainly used for training purposes, naturally housing hundreds of young naval recruits. Revis had a pintable installed in what was called a 'Vendo-Mat', a small building housing self-service food and drinks, dispensed by coin operated vending machines. Mainly used by the young junior ratings, our regular problem was being called out to replace vandalised smashed glass covers on the pintable, as well as fixing the coin mechanisms due to all kinds of counterfeit or foreign coins being tried out. Better still was attending Petty Officers 4 Mess across the road, presided over by a large red-bearded senior officer by the name of Henry. He and his fellow officers were a constant source of amusement, as we tended to linger longer than planned. In those years, a 'tot' of daily rationed navy rum was made available to serving sailors, up until 'Black Tot Day' on the 31st July 1970 when the practice was phased out. Henry often called our office to report non-existent 'problems' with the fruit machine – the 'one-armed bandit' that swallowed the old sixpences, providing a healthy profit for the mess as they had the keys as part of the rental agreement. Unlike modern machines, there were no built-in security measures that logged every single cash input or pay-outs, so one can only imagine where a lot of coins ended up in the day! As soon as we rolled up, the rum came out as we sat around the table, chatting away and telling bawdy jokes – the likes of which would cause heart attacks with some of the modern PC brigade!

We enjoyed the hospitality, but not drinking as much as we would have liked, due to other jobs to cover. The breathalyser test was not yet in force, thus avoiding Colin being pulled over. He was also able to afford to buy and run a beautiful yellow 1930s Rolls Royce, which raised a few eyebrows as this was quite an expensive hobby for a man of moderate means. The suspicions were soon allayed, as he managed to make money out of the car for weddings and other special occasions.

The mess also rented a pintable, to which they had the keys to the cashbox, also enabling them to open the back cover on the top of the machine, giving access to the main back panel with display board, flashing lights and the numerical score windows. This particular model featured a cartoon scene, resembling a swish top floor hotel nightclub, with assorted champagne-swilling toffs at the bar. When the pinball was released onto the game board, the player had to use their flippers to guide it toward any high-scoring target, racking up the points etc. Located smack in the middle of the display image was an elevator door, which opened to reveal a drunken tramp, clearly gate-crashing this posh 'do'. This particular target button was worn out, with peeling paint, due to constant 'attacks' by the sailors.

Henry's mess was responsible for the highest cash yield on any pintable for miles around, by sticking pornographic photos on the image behind the doors, which slid open for about five seconds, thus giving the player and onlookers a good laugh! He replaced these 'dirty postcards' every week to provide the next round of constant play, with ensuing record takings. Unfortunately, this great money-spinning idea came to an abrupt end, following a special social function night in the Mess. A visiting Admiral and his wife had been invited for a meal, drinks and convivial chat in the usual manner. The Admiral's wife, a very refined well-spoken woman, had apparently never played on one of these amusement machines before , so took out a sixpence, then enjoyed herself as the ball shot around the game board. Yes – you've guessed. The much-aimed for target was miraculously hit, causing the lift doors to open, to reveal a highly graphic image from Henrys collection. The poor woman froze in her tracks, then quickly walked away to sit back at the dining table with a fixed expression on her face, although never mentioning the surprise to anyone on the night. Someone had forgotten to remove the photo, as well as leaving the machine plugged in. The mains plug was then discreetly disconnected before any other visitor stumbled across the shock display.

Whenever we had to replace any fruit machines, it was a case of attending the venue in order to empty the remaining cash from the payout tubes or the tempting jackpot window at the front that enticed the gamblers, being full of coins to whet the appetite. It was usually a club steward who kept a close eye on us, as we handed him the main cashbox to provide the venue's income, then proceeded to click the levers that allowed the rest of the sixpences to drop into the tray below. What they didn't realise was that the 'bandit' had a rear reserve tube full of coins, which was always overlooked. I seem to recall that this 'secret' tube was miraculously empty by the time the fruit machine arrived back at the workshop....

I have clear vivid memories of so many hilarious episodes in my long life, still making me - and others laugh when retelling the stories. One of them was when we had to repair a 'bandit' at the Royal Southern Yacht Club in Hamble, across the road from the Bugle pub on the narrow High Street. We had been left on our own, having fixed a small problem, before locking the machine up, handing the keys back to the barman on duty. As Colin walked across the dance floor, a cascade of coins flowed from his trouser bottoms, leaving a shiny trail in his wake. He had not realised that a big hole in one of his pockets had allowed this unexpected 'jackpot' to have dropped. Luckily, nobody noticed as the club was closed for the afternoon, allowing us to quickly scoop up the loot, with a quick exit, just like a latter day 'Bonnie and Clyde'. If we had been apprehended, then Colin would have simply brushed it away by explaining that this cache had merely been in his pocket from an earlier visit elsewhere. Fortunately, CCTV cameras were not in widespread use at that time.

Reg Bicknell was keen on getting me out on the road, so very kindly paid for my driving lessons, followed by my first test which I failed. The examiner was an elderly straight-faced ex-military type, so I anticipated a degree of 'resistance' in his judgement. I tucked my long wetted-down hair into my collar, with a polo neck sweater to further help the illusion. Despite a competent confident drive, the miserable bastard marked me down on some insignificant minor lapse of concentration, but a second test saw me pass with flying colours a few weeks later. A rather attractive lady examiner seemed to like me, sliding into the passenger seat, with her clipboard ready to see if I was good enough to be let loose on the nation's roads. The fact that she was wearing a short skirt might have caused another distraction, but I used a degree of self-control, keeping my mind focussed on the next thirty minutes!

Before gaining my licence, whenever Colin was away on holiday, or not feeling well, it then fell to Reg to drive me out to assist with any service calls, as his eyesight was not too good. The bonus being that he had always owned a succession of flash cars, with a Borgward Isabella plus a Facel vega parked up next to his main pride and joy. This was a beautiful navy blue 1960 Ferrari 250 GT with white leather upholstery, plus a registration plate of OEV 1. From a distance, the number looked like DEV 1, so if an added 'L' was available at that time, then I'm sure he would have purchased it! If this car is still around these days, it would probably fetch somewhere between £8-

10m at a classic car auction. Just out of mild curiosity, I did a quick check on the OEV 1 plate on the DVLA website, noting that it takes pride on an Aston Martin, so still carrying on with the prestige. A second check on DEV 1 L, which would have possibly been available on a 1972 registration drew a blank, presuming that it would be to 'controversial'. However, the odd registration number release had passed under the scrutiny of the censors, especially a plate I recently noticed on a car parked at a Birmingham hotel. The number is currently on sale for £100,000, being appropriated by a classic vehicle registration company. It has raised many smiles over many years, as well as 'offending' the more sensitive types, so keep a look out for it if passing by - PEN 15. I anticipate a hard sell....

Reg was obviously too vain to wear glasses, which often caused us a few hiccups in our workshop when having problems with an electrical circuit on a pintable. Reg would roll up, start fiddling with the wiring, with squinting eyes that could not really focus on it. He soon gave up, saying *"F***k it – you two sort it out!"* before dashing back to the office. His main secretary was Marion Feltham, who has remained a good friend ever since those Revis days. She was also instrumental in finding me a couple of great used cars a little later, with family connections in the motor trade. Another secretary was Pat, who soon left to start a family, then replaced by a pretty young redhead, by the name of Glenda. Within a very short time, she had become ensconced in Reg's larger luxury house in Chilworth, a luxurious suburb on the edge of town known as 'Millionaires' Row. There was a quite an age gap, but they were happy together for a number of years, as well as giving Reg a spring in his step. I really liked him, as he had a great personality with a good business brain and was always very fair with his staff.

Glenda Marion

Having just passed my test, it was time for me to give up motorbikes for my first car, forking out the princely sum of £35 (around £500 these days). A complete rip-off, being a 1953 Ford Consul, registration 208 SMX (I only remember my first old bangers' number plates) purchased from Blishen Car Sales in Bedford Place. This turned out to be a nightmare, using more oil than petrol, so quickly off-loaded in part exchange for a much better late 50s Vauxhall Cresta (RDD 302) priced at £45. I always went for larger 'American' style automobiles, as this black beauty with handy front bench seats, plus another column gear-stick. As in 'handy' when taking girls out for a spin and much more....

THE SUMMER OF LOVE – 1967

Ask anyone of my age group if they had a favourite year. I bet most would agree with my own personal choice, as the latest cycle of popular music rolled across the Big Pond. Back in Southampton, I have more wonderful memories of the 'hippy' movement, linked to anti-war and general feeling of spreading peace and love. Maybe it was just the naivety of youth, but it felt good at the time. Hot summer days saw a bunch of us sitting in the park behind the old Tourist Information Kiosk with handy toilets, opposite the Civic Centre buildings. Chatting away, playing guitars as we sat on the grass - some were smoking 'grass' with a watchful eye for any passing policemen, but nobody ever bothered us, apart from the odd drunk staggering past with a mouthful of abuse at the *"Scruffy long-haired hippy f*****s"* sprawled on the ground. Many of us also hitch-hiked to nearby beaches, spending the weekend at places like Lepe or Barton-on-Sea on the edge of the New Forest, or even as far as Bournemouth, where we tucked into sleeping bags, with several 'Love-Ins' going on! You may notice that, throughout this book, I refrain from naming any of my old girlfriends as a matter of respect, so no 'kiss and tell' comes into play, but I can still picture them all with precious memories of a young single lad.

When my previous Unforgiven group had been booked into the Army bases near Salisbury during 1965, I was discreetly approached by a guy, employed as a civilian driver for the services. 'Big Ted' Vaughan was a giant of a man, who also worked as a bouncer on local doors of pubs and clubs, with a reputation for sorting any trouble out within seconds - either by his intimidating size, diplomatic talk or resorting to using his massive fists as a last resort! He was a very funny ruddy-faced inhabitant of Durrington Walls, a small village on the edge of Salisbury Plain, with a wonderful Wiltshire accent to match. Ted had a love for the music, being in the process of looking after a newly-formed group, who were looking for a lead singer. Apart from the fact that I was more than happy with my current pals, I had no wish to move out to that remote area, some 35 miles from my Woolston home, with over an hour's journey time, so politely declined. Despite our family not having a telephone at home, Ted somehow tracked me down a couple of years later, to see if I was still interested in joining his 'Cellars of Sound' a nice pun. I was in between groups at the time, apart from jamming with a couple of line-ups that didn't work out, so thought I'd give it a go.

I drove up to meet and rehearse with this new outfit, which worked out very quickly, leading to several bookings all over the county and beyond. Lead guitarist was 'Pip' Doris, with Richie Bull on bass, Mick Harvey on rhythm guitar plus Dave Maggs on percussion. Ted's army connections worked very well, being able to get us into the bases, which were reasonably well paid at that time. Most of these venues being officers' Messes or at large Summer Balls, which carried on through the night into the early hours.

Irony is a great word, especially when I think of those army shows at which many of the squaddies mirrored our own stage clothes. It was quite amusing to see these tough soldiers dressed up in kaftans, with beads, bells and even flowers in their short hair – well at best stuck behind their ears as heads were generally shaved! The walls had been decorated with 'Peace and Love' signs with images of flowers all around, some of them blowing soap bubbles as if they were prancing round in a San Francisco park. They were always receptive audiences, but we had to laugh over the harsh reality of what they would all do next morning, after sobering up. It would be straight back into training and manoeuvres on the nearby Army ranges, being taught how to kill people by unarmed combat or blasting the enemy with guns, rockets and tanks! So much for 'Make Love – Not War'…..

These shows exhausted me, resulting in a couple of hours' sleep, after a late drive home, then up early for the day job, unless on a weekend. I sometimes stopped over with Ted's family to break the journey, or if we had a show on the following night. His wife Winnie and their two children looked after me on these visits, so I was another nice period in my eventful life on the road. The Cellars also had the luxury of an old van to transport us and the equipment around, often serving as temporary overnight 'digs' if working at some distance. This made sense if we were booked on consecutive nights in the same area, so not worth traipsing back to base. As you know, one of my regrets is not having that many of photographs from my 64-72 group days, except for a few rare pictures that I took, as my interest in photography was building. This image shows us on Weymouth Beach, the day after we had performed a show at the massive Pavilion nearby, but left the gear there overnight. This then gave us all the chance to sleep - or try to sleep in the van parked up on the road behind, as shown in the photo. Many groups across the country will testify that they resorted to this same uncomfortable 'accommodation', as our paltry fees, less petrol and agency commissions would see us out of pocket if having the luxury of a cheap B&B for the night. Who cared – it was a giggle.

The Cellars of Sound - Mobile 'Hotel' in the background

Front row- 'Pip', Richie Mick
Back row – the two Daves

This stopover was another in a long line of crazy nights, which saw five sweaty lads and manager pile into the van for the night ahead. Personal hygiene went out of the window, following a long hot day in travelling down to the coast in the old jalopy, without the modern luxury of air-conditioning, apart from opening a window, if not broken. We then had to offload the amps and drums, followed by an active show with me leaping about all over the stage, before packing the gear up, in readiness to be picked up the next morning when the building opened. No showers available, so straight into the van for more laughs, filthy jokes then attempting to catch a few hours of blissful sleep. No chance, as the night was punctuated with snoring, coughing and farting contests, as a result of eating fish and chips or burgers from a dodgy junk food kiosk in the vicinity. Body odour and smelly feet all added to the toxic atmosphere, but none of us really cared at that age. I would do it all over in a flash if possible, just so good to look back at times like this.

We were looked upon as a 'psychedelic' group in those times, our set list reflecting the changes of that innovative year, culminating in the June release of 'Sgt Pepper's Lonely Hearts Club Band' which defined the decade. I wish I had the foresight to have kept the lists of songs from each of my different groups across those 8 years, on top of taking photos – few of us bothered, but I'm sure that many fans would have taken their own, but maybe lost or stashed away in a shoebox somewhere. A couple of our favourite numbers stick in my mind, with the Move's 'I Can Hear the Grass Grow' plus the Stones' 'Let's Spend the Night Together' amongst the standard tracks accumulated over the years. It was a superb band, but the constant travelling was getting me down, as I was losing sleep as well as having the hassle of being late for my day job, or trying to get away early to dash off for an evening gig.

I broke the news to the Cellars, who all suggested that I should move out to their area, which was not an option for me, as I was still living at home with few outgoings. All of my family and friends would be left behind, so it was not feasible. In addition, my old car was not very reliable, with a few breakdowns that caused a few problems whenever I had to cover this long distance trek to meet up with the lads etc. Ted was distraught at hearing this news, but then offered to help the situation with an incredible idea which I found very humbling and have never forgotten. His solution was to drive down to my home, pick me up then drive back to Salisbury Plain in readiness for the evening show. When we all got back to base in the early hours, this then saw Ted taking me all the way to Southampton. I didn't think this was fair on him, as he worked hard all day long with his day job, followed by another full evening by driving us all over the place. He insisted that it would be fine, but I knew that it would result in a loss of his own sleep, after any show. I reluctantly agreed to this agreement, but not for long as I felt embarrassed by it all so it was time for me to move on.

Ted with son Michael outside their house

I'm not sure how long the Cellars carried on following my departure, but drummer Dave Maggs later joined the Andover-based Troggs around 1988, touring the world with them until his recent departure in 2018. This was a great thirty year run for him, but no surprise, being one of the best percussionists in the business. We met up a few years ago when the Troggs headlined a travelling Sixties show at Birmingham's Symphony Hall. I had a backstage pass, so good to meet up with him again after so many years, as well as joining him and the band across the road as we naturally hit the pub after the gig! Black Sabbath guitarist Tony Iommi was also there to meet up with his old mates, giving me a chance to talk to him, plus grabbing a photo together! Maggsy not looking too happy, after having his phone stolen from the dressing room on the night.

Two Daves

Lead singer Reg Presley was fun, chatting about his well-documented passion for UFOs, crop circles, alchemy, lost civilisations plus all manner of eccentric stuff. Late in life, he had a massive bonus over his song-writing talents, which had provided him with a good 'pension' stemming from their big hits of the mid Sixties. They were very basic, but catchy which is what it's all about in the pop music industry. Much bigger royalty cheques came his way, thanks to one of his old compositions being taken up as part of the soundtrack for two blockbuster movies. 'Four Weddings And A Funeral' followed by 'Love Actually' made use of Reg's 1968 hit of 'Love Is All Around' given a superb arrangement by Wet Wet Wet. Their version stayed on the number one spot for fifteen weeks, a record at that time before overtaken by Bryan Adam's 'Everything I Do' with a sixteen weeks slot. Having sold nearly 2m units so far, it certainly boosted Reg's bank balance for a few years until his passing in 2013 at the age of 71.

Mr Presley!

Anyone who was ever lucky enough to be part of a pop group would tell you that, apart from the fun of it all, at the back of our young minds was harbouring a dream that maybe some day we would be 'spotted' by a talent scout. One really had to be very 'different' or possess a great voice, as well as being in or near London, as this is where it all happened. My song writing talents never took off, dabbling with lyrics, accompanied by my guitar or piano at home. The first efforts sounded good, but then reality came in as I soon recognised similar-sounding hits from before – a common problem as many will endorse. Television was always in my sights, especially when watching 'Opportunity Knocks' that was discovering new talent, so time for me to have another stab at stardom as a solo singer. The application form was filled in, sent off with a reply after a few weeks, offering an audition at the Skyway hotel near the new Southampton Docks. I checked in, sat around for a short while amongst the other hopefuls, before my name was called out, then ushered into the function room

Po-faced TV host Hughie Green with the stern production staff sat at a long table, taking notes as I told the grumpy piano player of my choice of song, which I still remember as a current hit of that year. Paul Jones had left Manfred Mann by then, carving out a solo career as an actor/singer. He starred in a 1967 movie 'Privilege' about a megalomaniac pop star, from which I had chosen one of the released singles from the soundtrack. The song was 'I've Been A Bad, Bad

Boy' but I wasn't fully prepared by not having the sheet music for the elderly pianist, who had never heard of it, being a current release. He grimaced when I asked if he could 'busk' it, attempting to follow me after finding which key I was singing in. Needless to say, Green and co. were not impressed, so the expected *"Thank you – we'll be in touch..."* was the answer, but I didn't break down in tears like some modern day wannabe, with a shattered 'dream' or some heart-rending sob story that often forms part of the 'Reality TV, circus! I merely shrugged it off, thinking that I might try and get 'on the box' at some later stage in my life, little knowing that I would manage it by another very unusual 'trivial' avenue in 1982....

THE END - NOT QUITE...

Woolston was a really nice suburb to grow up in, with a 'village; feel that still resonates today, although the main shopping streets have changed, as well as the major development of the Itchen Bridge, opened in 1977. This resulted in the demolition of several homes and shops to make way for the access roads on both sides of the new route into town. Traffic arriving from the city side pass through the toll booths, leading directly onto Portsmouth Road eventually heading eastbound and out of the area. Just on the right stands one of the oldest pubs in the area, renamed the Cricketers Arms, harking back to its original 19th Century name, due to having the old Hampshire Cricket Club ground to the rear. It was recently known as the Bridge Inn, following on from the New Bridge Inn, linked to the new access across the River Itchen. It was our family's local pub, giving me the opportunity to sit in the beer garden on warm summer days, as well as being offered stealthy sips of my father's shandy. During the Fifties, it had been named the Railway Hotel with its proximity to the nearby station, before another change to the Woolston.

By 1968 I was on the lookout for my next band, checking out any local musos who might be looking for a new front man. My recent day jobs had seen me employed as a delivery driver for a couple of local firms, having left Revis Automatics, but my evenings saw me at a loss due to not being on a stage somewhere. Odd weekends saw me and my pals having a drink at the Woolston, with the bonus of watching the resident group in action, fronted by one of Southampton's longest rock'n'roll singers in the shape of Tex Roberg. He was formerly labelled 'The South African Elvis' migrating to Southampton in the late Fifties, where he soon became well established as one of the top acts around. Good-looking, with a great voice and stage presence, topped off with a sun-tanned torso underneath a white string vest that captivated the ladies! April 1962 had seen Tex Roberg and the Graduates opening up the show at Hamburg's new Star Club, after winning the toss of a coin with the Beatles!

In between Tex's odd breaks through the night, the band invited any guest singers to get up for a few numbers, so I naturally obliged. I slotted in well with the lads, one of whom being Eastleigh's Graham Medley - my old mate from the 1965 Unforgiven group. With Tony Burnett on drums plus guitarist Roy Perry, it all clicked with my own songs, harmonica and messing about. It soon became apparent that Tex was not too enamoured with this young pretender who was getting more attention from the audience, leading to a degree of resentment. I had to laugh at a bit of 'sabotage' on one of my guest slots, as the p.a. system amplifier was located out of sight, in the wings of the function room stage. Tex had taken a breather in that small area, resulting in the volume mysteriously cutting out during my performance, much to everybody's amusement. It was pretty obvious what was going on, but we all laughed it off as part of the game. Within a very short time, Tex decided to leave the group, allowing me to step into his blue suede shoes, so to speak. This latest move saw the start of my last four years in this avenue of the business, with even more fun and games that saw the pub packed over the weekend. Our new name became The Script for the first three years, as we settled into the new phase of psychedelia and heavier style of music.

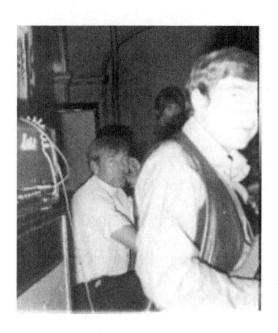

Tony Burnett   Roy Perry

The landlady at that time was Doris 'Dolly' Wheatman, a large woman who sat on her own barstool all night long, sipping whisky whilst keeping a close eye on who was coming through the front entrance. We were entertaining the punters in the large function room on a tiny stage, later extended into a small add-on so giving me more space to mess about. The strict licensing laws only allowed a maximum of two musicians on the stage, which explained why Doll was on high alert through these show nights, in case any officials decided to pay a surprise visit to check on the back room. She had a switch on the bar, wired through to a warning light above our heads, so a quick flick gave us the nod. Guitarists Roy and Graham quickly moved out of sight to their side of the stage, hiding in the wings, leaving me and Tony who just drummed away on his own for a while, making out it was a long solo! I just sat down by the side or jumped into a nearby seat to allow one of the others to walk back on to make it look like the prescribed duo at work.

Graham Medley

Everybody sang, so gave us plenty of scope to cover a wide range of songs plus good harmony vocals. We also had a few laughs by swapping instruments during a long number without missing a beat – akin to musical chairs. Apart from the standard pop, rock'n'roll, R&B stuff, we were also moving with the times, including more progressive music that was creeping in. Luckily, I managed to retain our old set list book, the only record of all of my 64-72 group music information, which makes for interesting reading. Apart from our main Woolston pub gig, the band was also booked for various outside shows, mainly via Avenue Artistes Agency, with other local musicians filling in for us. We were never worried about them sneaking in to usurp us, due to our strong following and a faithful fan base. Many of our main supporters were local bikers, whose beautiful machines were parked up on the pavement at the front of the pub, providing a good meeting point for them all. One or two of them always stayed outside, keeping an eye for any passing Mods who might be tempted to kick one over or worse, as there was still a degree of animosity between the two camps.

Roy Perry

Money-wise, it was a complete rip-off as 'Dolly' was as tight as the proverbial duck's arse, despite our resident status pulling in large crowds over the three nights. We were only paid £8 each for the whole weekend, with a few polite requests for a slight rise being met with a stubborn refusal. I was never unduly worried about this parsimonious set-up, as it was countered by the convenience of simply walking a few hundred yards to the pub from our house, plus not having to load equipment, then travel long distances as in previous years on the road. To boost our meagre wages, we often staged special themed nights, with a small door charge to give us a few more quid in our pocket, although we generally spent much of it across the bar when playing all night. A record player was also set in the wings, to play discs for the breaks as well as being used for any miming gimmicks that we incorporated into the act.

One of these early themed nights include my rendition of a no. 1 hit recorded by the eccentric Crazy World of Arthur Brown, whose 1968 recording of 'Fire' had a major impact. His appearances on live shows saw him wearing a flaming head-dress, as part of the whole Satanic profile. I wasn't prepared to go that far, as the poor man suffered for his art due to simply wearing a leather skull cap with a metal container full of inflammable liquid, leading to painful scalp burns! We had the record on the turntable, in readiness for my entrance as the other lads left the stage for this next treat. On the front of the stage extension, were placed two burning cauldrons (old black painted cake tins) containing firelighters with petrol added to provide a healthy looking flame, enhanced by the room lights being extinguished. The strong smelling fumes were not appreciated by those sitting at the front, these tables having been taken as soon as the doors were open with a mad scramble to the stage area. Shirtless, dressed in a long black cape, with scary black make-up applied to my chest and face was the first glimpse as I slowly walked to the pull-out stage block, staring with 'mad' eyes around the audience. The stylus then hit the record groove, belting out this amazing track that I was about to mime to, as it only had an Hammond organ backing with no guitars on the actual recording, augmented by a brass section so impossible for us to recreate live.

"I am the God of Hell Fire....and I give you – Fire!" was the opening line, then lip-syncing the whole track, gyrating in a mad frenzy as per Arthur Brown's antics, as seen on Top of the Pops and other television shows of that time. Unbeknown to the audience, I had some loose gunpowder to hand, obtained from fireworks, throwing small handfuls into the burning containers throughout the song. Massive flares ensued followed by plumes of white smoke drifting over the heads of the crowd, but there was worse to come. I had been drinking a few beers throughout the night, so my judgement was slightly impaired as I grabbed another handful of powder – a bigger one than planned. This next addition resulted in a loud bang, with a massive twelve foot flame leaping up to the low polystyrene ceiling tiles, some of which promptly caught on fire. Luckily, we had the

presence of mind to have a fire extinguisher on standby, which was quickly utilised to spray the burning panels much to everybody's relief. This did not stop me from carrying on with the full mime, leading to a great applause from the room, followed by a telling-off by the irate landlady who had no idea what had been planned. This was talked about for a long time after, but banned, never to be repeated. Can you imagine if we had 'health and safety' around at that time? We considered our shows to be a form of 'theatrical rock' which was taken to bigger levels by the likes of Alice Cooper and others, albeit on much bigger stages than ours.

On 'normal' nights, we often got up to more mischief by enhancing a few numbers with various ideas. One included singing the old spiritual 'Jailer Bring Me Water' as if I was dying of thirst, dropping down on my knees, begging for something to drink. This 'request' saw one of the girls approaching the stage with a soda syphon, aiming for my open mouth. Needless to say, I got fully drenched, before running off to get changed back into dry clothes. Another popular request was for 'The Ballad of Bonnie and Clyde', a 1967 hit for Georgie Fame, telling the story of the 1930s American gangster couple. The ending of the hit record was a volley of machine gun fire, recreating the police ambush leading to the deaths of the fugitives. Drummer Tony provided this sound effect by a rapid snare drum fill, as I writhed all over the stage, with the 'bullets' finding their target, then sliding off onto the floor below at the feet of the amused onlookers. The microphone was then handed down to me as I gasped my dying breaths to deliver the last line of the song before slumping in a dead heap. All part of the fun and games.

EASY RIDER

As you can well imagine, the Woolston pub was the talk of the town, as no other local group were doing what we did. Our much-talked about gimmicks were an extension of the act, which was good anyway by featuring excellent musicians who had all been playing for many years with other top outfits. Adding contemporary tracks by the likes of The Doors, Vanilla Fudge, Family, Spooky Tooth and similar music provided even more variety, as we really entertained the customers. For us it was a step from a straightforward musical performance, enjoyed from both sides of the stage.

On a personal level, I had left my job as an amusement machine service engineer, followed by a couple of odd driving jobs, providing a steady income. One of these was driving a van for Gardiners Tool Company near Bevois Valley, delivering goods to hardware shops from Southampton up through Berkshire and Oxfordshire. I quite enjoyed being alone on the road, with plenty of opportunity to take loads of breaks as many skivers did in those days. No tachographs or mobile phones, so complete freedom to enjoy long tea breaks throughout the day. A similar job followed on, by working a similar job for Tillings Ship Chandlers in St Michael's Square opposite the Silhouette Night Club/Casino owned by Brian 'Kiwi' Adamson. You may be aware that he commissioned me to write his incredible life story, which can be found on my Amazon author page. My main duty was driving a pick-up truck all over the South coast, carrying marine equipment, so another easy period of employment. During the Sixties, it was simple to leave one employment, then straight into a new one the next day – how times changed later on

This new residency coincided with my purchase of a dream car, thanks to Marion Feltham of Revis Car Sales and Automatics, whose father ran a scrapyard as well as dealing in second hand vehicles. For the princely sum of £70 (£1200) I was the proud owner of a 1960 Ford Consul convertible, with a white body and red stripe along the side panels. Fake leopard skin seat covers and a red hood set it all off, plus a roomy front bench seat thanks to another column gear shift. Registration number 930 CKC sticks in my mind to this day, as it does with Marion who always reminds me of that time when she first saw it, saying *"I know the very person that would suit this posing car!"* It was very reliable and a joy to drive in all weathers, especially with the roof down. Unfortunately, I don't have many photos of this favourite car. A short while later, I had a bonnet mascot fixed in the shape of a jet plane, sourced from a scrapped Chevrolet, setting it all off. The Consul also made the long journey to Cornwall, for a week's camping holiday with a girlfriend and a family I knew well.

Our next blockbuster show was a themed Rock'n'Roll night, leading to another surprise that took the roof off, but not using gunpowder this time round. Again, a few quid taken on the door helped to augment the pittance paid by Mrs Scrooge, as we called her, leading to another packed room that often exceeded the fire regulations capacity which nobody ever bothered about. We kicked off with a non-stop high octane show of classic 50s hits before having a short break.

A large heavy plank of thick wood was carried through the crowd, then propped onto the stage front, causing much curiosity with the fans, having no idea what was coming. We got back on stage, clad in borrowed leather jackets, as the entrance double doors were opened to the sound of two magnificent café racer motorbikes that had been noisily ridden in through the main pub door leading from the road. One of my old mates, Keith Walshe, was riding his beloved Spruce Green Triton 650cc T110 with American straight inline twin carburettors, chromed Norton chain-case (unusual for then). His pal Reg McIntyre followed him on his purple Bonneville 650, as the confused bar regulars had to move apart to make way through the crowd.

The bikes slowly threaded their way through the outer lounge bar, much to the consternation of the landlady, perched on her stool as she immediately knocked back another large whisky to calm her nerves at the sight. The lads then manoeuvred their machines through the closely packed room, as a pathway was cleared in order for them to reach the plank, ride up onto the stage, before handing control of one of them to me. One of my favourite cult movies was the 1969 'Easy Rider' starring Peter Fonda and Dennis Hopper, playing a couple of drug-crazed bikers, riding Harley Davidsons across America. The brilliant soundtrack included Steppenwolf's 'Born To Be Wild' which has become a bikers' anthem ever since with a thumping beat that heralded the early influences of later classic rock around the end of that decade. Serious rock fans will know that the term 'heavy metal' was first heard in the lyrics of this very song as the 2nd verse has the line *"I like smoke and lightnin' - heavy metal thunder."*

Keith & cousin on that Norton

We launched into this classic song, with me sitting astride the heavy beast, the engine still running, made even louder as I revved it up, resulting in clouds of black exhaust fumes sweeping across the front rows and filling the room. A few people were choking by now, so were relieved that it was only a short number, otherwise it might have resulted in a serious case of carbon monoxide poisoning! Once again, this mad idea was never allowed to be repeated much to the disappointment of us all. A dark fog swarmed all around the room until handing back control of the bikes, which were then ridden down the ramp and out the back doors leading to the pub car park. We had to leave the double crash doors open to get some fresh air back to the masses for a good while, as well having more laughs when hearing about Reg dropping the bike out the back, due to posing away with wheel spins! The audience kept laughing when I had to announce to people to stop drinking, as small drops of a black oily liquid had appeared on the top of their glasses. The mystery was solved when discovering that this was due to the Castrol R fuel additive pumped out of the exhaust pipes!

There were also a few girls in regular attendance who were labelled 'easy riders' but I draw a veil over that side of what we call the business of sex, drugs and rock'n'roll. I only admit to two of them, although many people swear that I must have been "on something" to explain many of my stage antics. My kicks were simply the buzz and the adrenalin of entertaining the crowds as well as myself. I thank Keith for reminding me of the above information, which will appeal to classic bike enthusiasts as well as him sending a recent pic to show that real Rock'n'Rollers never die!

Keith Walshe

Another of my ideas had to be kept under wraps to avoid the wrath of the landlady, or in case the local authorities caught wind of what we planned. I had often travelled up to London on day trips with my best pal Pete, either by train or by car for an overnight sleep in Regents Park next to the Zoo. We had great times walking around the West End, especially enjoying the buzz of Carnaby Street at its height during the daytime. Evenings were spent wandering around Soho, with the odd visit to a strip club as one does at that age. This gave me an idea to book a stripper for one of our special nights at the Woolston, managing to find a list of London-based girls who were willing to travel down for a one-off show. We glossed over the actual act making out that we were featuring a guest 'dancer', keeping it under wraps until the night before when I made a thinly- disguised stage announcement, with a wink and a nod, so that the regulars knew what was coming.

The big day came, as I drove over to the main Central Station to pick the lady up, feeling relieved to find out that she was very attractive, unlike some of the dodgy strippers we had seen back in Soho! She was a few years older than me, which didn't hinder my mild chatting up on the way back to the pub, not reciprocated but worth a try. She was really nice and friendly, impressing Doll when entering the pub on the way to a changing room elsewhere in the building.

As anticipated, the function room was jam packed with a mixed audience, but mainly lads who had pushed their way down to the front of our stage, in anticipation. Our guest 'exotic dancer' had to be onstage fairly early, in order to get back home on a late train so around 9pm I announced our special guest. The band played her on with her requested music, as she shimmied through the crowds to cheers and wolf-whistles all the way to the stage. Doll was on her usual perch in the next bar, whisky in hand with her beady eye on the main outside entrance door, but completely unaware of what 'entertainment' was really happening behind our closed doors.

She was very classy, performing a slow sensuous act, throwing each outer garment to me as I was conveniently sat by the side of the stage to catch her clothes. She was not able to move through the

125

packed audience but managed to tease both the lads and girls sat at the front, before putting her cape back for the final part of her show. The G string dropped to the floor, then kicked over to me for safe keeping, followed by letting the cape fall to the floor, with a full frontal reveal of her charms! As you can imagine, the crowd went wild - the men were cheering, stamping their feet with a constant loud whistling, along with open-mouthed girls who could not believe what they had probably just witnessed for the first time.

It was time for a hasty dash to take her back to the station, the band carrying on with their own music for a short while. A nice farewell, with just a kiss on the cheek as she boarded her London train. I drove straight back to finish off the evening, as well as facing the wrath of 'Doll' who had gone ballistic when learning of what had just gone on – or come off! She could have lost her licence over this infringement, but it was hardly 'obscene' as such, although striptease was not part of the allowed entertainment which covered music and dancing. She was an 'exotic dancer' so this may have provided some defence before the authorities, although classified as a public performance. Once again, this was never repeated as Doll kept a close eye on any future 'special' shows, wanting to know every minor detail of our plans.

THE HEIGHT OF MY CAREER?

We all do silly things in life that we often regret, but looking back with a smile as I do when remembering a change of employment that could have ended my life at the age of twenty. Back at the Woolston pub, a tall slim guy always stood quietly on his own at the back, next to the door. I got chatting to 'Mac' as he was known, when the conversation turned to talking about jobs. He surprised me when finding out that his unusual employment was a steeplejack of all things, which I found fascinating. He then asked if I was working, as he was looking for someone to help him out on a few jobs but could never find anyone who would be prepared to take on such a risky occupation. Most people have a fear of heights anyway, but I didn't really know if I was in that category. I was intrigued by his offer, plus the fact that the pay was much higher than my boring driving job, so I thought - why not? The firm was based in a large house on Shrubbs Hill Road, Lyndhurst on the edge of the New Forest, where we picked up the daily worksheet and materials needed.

I have never had any major phobias as well as being fairly confident with most things in life, but I was a little apprehensive when arriving at my first trial. This was at a small factory near Winchester, being a basic routine maintenance job on the tall chimney. Fortunately this latest caper was during the summer months, so quite pleasant weather to go for my first climb up the ladder that Mac had already fixed some time before. He gave me some basic training on the ground before inviting me up to the dizzy heights above. I started to ascend, grabbing the rungs tightly as well as not looking down too much as this might have reversed my lack of nerves. It only took a few minutes to reach the 'flying stage' a centuries-old method of providing a platform from which workmen could stand on, then fix the various support ropes to the metal safety rail around the perimeter. We only wore old light summer clothing as the work was rather messy, much of which was to lower ourselves down from the top to render the brickwork, clean and paint it with preservatives. This is where it all got scary as I had to climb onto a wooden 'bosun's chair – more or less a child's swing fixed by ropes to the platform above. No safety harness, helmet, hi-viz jacket or any other protection that we take for granted these days. It was then a case of a slow abseil down the chimney, with feet resting on the brickwork, dipping my large brush into the paint can hooked onto the end of my uncomfortable seat. What was I thinking? I had to have full confidence in Mac's attention to detail as he was fully responsible for overseeing every aspect for both our sakes. He reassured me that my ropes were securely fixed, so no need to worry about a thing, but at the back of my mind the negative thoughts were running wild. My life was literally in his hands.

The views were good, but the actual work was more or less labouring, which never appealed to me. I only lasted a few weeks in that precarious job, after navigating a few more chimneys and a church spire, so I handed my notice in. Another factor being that I did some research on steeple-jacking, then realised how many fatalities were recorded in the high risk trade, usually by negligence, faulty equipment or a mere lack of concentration for a few seconds. A couple of days before I left, we were travelling through Salisbury, which led to Mac surprising me by turning into the Cathedral car park. He had access to many churches in the South, including this magnificent building, so I just thought he was going to show me around, as we were bunking off for a while so plenty of time to spare.

The next thing I knew was being let into a private area, through an old oak door leading to the first of several hundred steps. Mac then laughed at my puzzled expression, as he informed me that my going-away present was the long climb to the very top of the tallest church spire in the country! Luckily from the inside, as I would never have attempted to climb up ladders to reach the pointed roof at 404 feet! The first stone steps took us a long way up inside the stone walls, before reaching the cone – shaped section at the top. Then a final ascent up old wooden steps and ladders took us to the narrowest point, with a viewing window, overlooking miles of surrounding countryside. This was an incredible moment, but spoilt by not having a camera with me, to record this unique chance of a lifetime. We were both exhausted by the time we reached the ground, but it was well worth it for me. Looking back, it was a crazy reckless employment choice of mine by agreeing to give it a try in the first place, but remains yet another great memory of an exciting life, with never a dull moment, albeit a moment of madness!

I was also quite keen on taking photos by then, enabling me to grab a few shots of this latest group in action, as well as getting someone to use my camera in order that I could be in the frame. This explains the final images in these last chapters, not forgetting that I was careful to save so many precious memories.

'SCREAMING LORD CRUTCH!'

I guess by now that you have realised that I was – and still am rather eccentric whenever hitting any stage with the full intention of entertaining people, allowing them to forget any problems they may have. Popular music has often produced many off the wall characters, none more controversial than David 'Lord' Sutch aka 'Screaming Lord Sutch' whose own stage antics had always inspired me from the early Sixties. His 1963 release of 'Jack The Ripper' had been banned by the BBC, due to being in 'bad taste' glorifying the Whitechapel Murders of 1888 with its screams, sound effects and lyrics that some found disturbing. His live shows were a parody of horror themes plus all manner of hilarious over the top segments, in between his rock'n'roll singing, which left a lot to be desired. His early backing groups contained several future top name musicians, all of which can be found by simple web searches, so well worth a look. David had set up Radio Sutch, as part of the pirate radio phenomenon that beamed the best pop music from ships and disused WW2 defence towers outside the UKs territorial waters. I have referred to this in the early chapters, due to his association with impresario Reg Calvert, who took over the running of the station for a short while, Sutch wanting to be back on dry land for his nationwide live shows. He also stood as a parliamentary candidate in several local and national elections, gaining more notoriety with his crazy 'manifestos', under the name of the National Teenage Party from 1963. This later morphed into the Official Raving Monster Loony Party in 1983, leading to his setting a record as the longest-serving party leader of all time, regardless of losing some 40 elections!

This final choice of our themed nights took a while to plan, deciding that a tribute show to 'His Lordship' would be a laugh, as well as drawing the paying crowds through the doors. A makeshift 'coffin' was knocked up by my father John, who happened to be a carpenter, using an old scrapped wooden mini-bowling alley lane that I had procured from an amusement machine company. The outside was painted black with a large white cross on the lid, then stored in a back room of the pub in readiness for the big night. The band got together for a rehearsal, choosing the right kind of music to enhance the spectacle later that evening, which saw yet another capacity audience, which had queued for ages in the adjacent bar. We opened with our normal variable set list, before taking a break in readiness for what everybody was waiting for, but not really knowing what was in store for the front row seats. Roy, Tony and Graham took the stage at the same time I was climbing into the coffin in the next room, then held aloft by my 'pallbearers' in the shape of six burly bikers. The group struck up with Chopin's eerie Funeral March as the cortege made its way by pushing through the packed room, which took quite a while as I recall. I was then placed gently onto the stage, with a microphone handed into the box, ready to sing the first song. This was a classic number released way back in 1956 by weird American blues singer, calling himself 'Screaming' Jay Hawkins who had performed a similar stage act, as copied by Sutch. "I Put A Spell On You" was the perfect vehicle for me, singing the first verse before slowly moving the lid aside, climbing out of the coffin, dressed in a long black cape with top hat, moving stealthily around the stage.

The monster appears..

The music carried on as I then picked up a small glass of a green 'magic potion' (a liqueur) then clutching my throat in mock pain, in the mode of the Jekyll and Hyde 'transformation' story. I then staggered into the side area by the back of the stage, quickly donning a horror mask plus long bony rubber 'monster' hands before running back out into the audience, straight to the girls of course! A few of them actually screamed, adding to the atmosphere, or just cowered at the sight of me approaching their tables. The next part of the act saw me 'hypnotise' guitarist's wife Julie Perry, who stood up with glazed eyes, then up the steps as I beckoned her to lie down in the coffin for the shocking finale. Ripping my mask off, with 'I Put A Spell On You' giving way to Sutch's 'Jack The Ripper' cranked it all up into the unexpected climax of this mad evening.

Scary or what?

So good to be close to the crowd on these mad nights, especially the girls as we had quite a big fan base which came along night after night across these four years of mayhem.

The loud final music segment of Grieg's 'Hall Of The Mountain King' saw me pulling out a large knife, before seemingly plunging into the victim's prostrate body, although the audience could not see Julie laughing her head off as I went about the business to hand. Many of the squeamish onlookers grimaced as I had quickly smeared the blade with tomato ketchup, whilst in the act of cutting the body up, then holding it up to lick it all off. Not for the faint-hearted.

I had also secreted a bag of offal, purchased from the nearby butcher early that same day, leading to me grabbing pieces of meat and sheep eyes which were then thrown into the crowd – some of which were picked up and thrown back at me but all in fun. The show ended with me plunging the knife into my own stomach before slumping to the floor in a dead heap as the group played the final chord. I just stayed there for a while, milking the applause and cheering from the room, before taking a bow into another break, in order to clean up the bloody mess and clear the stage for the last part of the evening. This 'Ripping' show was intended to be a one-off, but had to be repeated a few months later by public demand as the word got out all over town.

A PICTURE OF YOU

I had been singing this 1962 Joe Brown hit for a while, as well as developing a keen interest in photography a few years later, all thanks to my father who had often taken pictures on his Box Brownie and a Kodak camera. Fortunately, he really looked after many of these photos which ended up in treasured albums that I still have to this day. Dad had a natural knack for taking really good photos, as I often look through them all, noticing how his technique produced lasting memories for me, during these 'twilight' years of my life.

Around 1969, I got to know Barry Kennett, who worked for another local amusement machine company, but was looking to set up a small business of his own, albeit in a different field. We were talking about photography in general, which was also one of his own hobbies. Barry was quite impressed with my work, suggesting that we form a partnership – only he invested the money, as I was always broke, but my new skills served as my part of the deal. We rented out a shop at 16 High Road in Swaythling, being one side of semi-detached houses, previously used as accommodation and storage for the shopkeepers before us. We came up with a name for our enterprise, calling it Nova Graphic as a 'new' venture, transforming the front area into an office. The two window displays contained large framed photographs, illustrating the general focus of our main business, which covered commercial, weddings, portraiture and other types of image requirements. We knocked out a partition wall to the rear of the building, creating a large studio space from the two small rooms, with the walls being painted in white. There was a small kitchen at the far end, with running water from a sink, giving us the perfect opportunity to convert it into a darkroom. These walls and ceiling were painted black, before installing the processing equipment such as an enlarger plus trays for developing our own B&W prints up to 10x8 size. Colour negatives had to be sent off to a local company, as the process was quite tricky and out of our comfort zone, as the materials were expensive, apart from the liquid temperatures needing to be within very strict parameters, resulting in wastage.

Amazingly enough, we only used 35mm cameras for our work, despite most companies using larger formats such as 120mm or 4x 5 plate cameras that were needed for larger prints, with top quality reproduction. It really was a very basic 'duck and dive' operation, but Barry's smooth salesmanship soon landed us with some work within a short time. Our main income came from offering family portraits taken in peoples' home settings, being a much more relaxed way of obtaining natural photographs. Childrens' pictures were very popular, although not always easy to get them to stay still and pose for the camera as any parent knows. We employed a couple of young girls who visited local housing estates, knocking on doors to sell our services on a commission basis. We then took the photos, developed a set of proofs which were taken back for orders from the customer with no upfront charges, apart from a small deposit to cover our basic costs in case none were wanted.

The turnover and profits were not as good as we had anticipated, leaving us with very little to invest in better equipment, with me only earning pocket money for the next couple of years, but we had fun in between. Many days saw us taking off to play snooker or just go for a drink somewhere, so the end was in sight. I fancied travelling over to attend the first Isle of Wight Festival in1969, with Bob Dylan headlining an amazing bill, so made advances to Portsmouth-based Fiery Creations, who had taken a big gamble on staging this ambitious event. The idea was for me to blag a press pass, authorising prime access all areas, in return for providing them with photographs, but this fell on deaf ears. I did manage to attend the following year, but as a paying customer, accompanied by my girlfriend, to witness another star-studded line-up of top acts with Jimi Hendrix at his peak. We pitched up around three hundred yards from the stage, but it still sounded good and loud with a wonderful atmosphere, much of it laced with cannabis fumes. I had been lucky to have seen Jimi close up at the Guildhall the year before, pushing my way to the front of the stage to witness the magic of the man.

We did make up our own (unofficial) press pass, used to good effect when waved at the door of concerts at the Guildhall, resulting in my grabbing some candid shots of Jethro Tull and The Who. There was little security in force at that time, unlike the modern strict practices so I often got in without paying, one of the best being when the Move came to town.

This amazing group hit the UK charts in 1967, soon becoming one of the most respected bands in the UK and across the world. They were another in a long line of 'Brumbeat' groups from Birmingham that were mounting a challenge to the sounds of 'Merseybeat' that had dominated the charts since the Beatles changed the music scene forever just a few years before. The Midlands provided such top bands as the Moody Blues, Fortunes, Rocking Berries and many more back in those heady days of the 'Swinging Sixties' but the Move were something special with 'attitude' plus great marketing skills that kept them on the front pages! Their stage act often featured such tactics as smashing TV sets to pieces, demolishing an old Cadillac plus being threatened with legal action by Prime Minister Harold Wilson, following a dodgy advertising promotion for 'Flowers In The Rain'. Pop fans will know that this was the first ever record to be played on the first Radio One show in 1967 (Tony Blackburn Show) and still sounds great after all these years!

As it happened, there had been a panic at the Guildhall for the Move concert, due to a local support band letting the venue down, so I quickly volunteered to scrape up a fill-in group to cover a short spot before the Move headlined. A couple of musician pals were already there, with a couple of hasty phone calls ensuring that my one-off group helped to save the day! It was all ad-libbed/unrehearsed, as I just shouted out the songs that I knew plus the key, so we just busked away! I was also playing my blues harmonica, noticing that Roy Wood was watching from the wings. When we came offstage, he congratulated us, complimenting me on my harp-playing, which made me feel very proud - I cheekily asked him if his band needed an extra singer/ harmonica player but he just laughed, saying that he'd keep me in mind!

Backstage, I asked the Move if I could take a couple of photographs for my personal collection, with my wish granted. Roy asked if I could send him any of these and gave me his home address of Streetly Road in Aldridge just outside of Birmingham. He also insisted on paying for them, despite my protestations to the contrary as I was so chuffed to have had the privilege as a big fan! I should have photocopied his cheque before banking it - an unusual piece of memorabilia I guess?

THE MOVE
Rick Price Roy Wood Carl Wayne Bev Bevan

Carl Wayne was one of the best lead vocalists in the music business, later launching a solo career when the Move broke up, followed by a short spell with the Hollies. Carl's health took a turn for the worse, but it never stopped him working right up to his untimely passing in 2004. Many people will not be aware that he married actress Sue Hanson - yes 'Miss Diane' of 'Crossroads' fame. Little did I know that I would eventually 'co-star' with her at the ATV/Central studios in Birmingham during the 80s (Alright - I only did some walk-on/extra work if you must know)

Carl Wayne 1943-2004

Drummer Bev Bevan later joined forces with Roy Wood's new line-up for his ambitious Electric Light Orchestra (later ELO fronted by Jeff Lynne) Roy then broke away to form Wizzard, later providing him with a seasonable 'pension' bonus by composing the 1973 'I Wish It Could be Christmas Everyday',annually earning nearly £200,000 in yearly royalty payments. Bev still plays with several different groups as well as presenting his Midlands radio shows.

Bass player Rick Price had a lower post-Move profile, with a producing and arranging career, as well as running his own recording studio. He also married singer Dianne Lee, of the chart-topping duo of Peters and Lee, following their discovery on Opportunity Knocks. Based in Somerset, they also perform as a duo around the South West with guest appearances on radio and television shows, linked to their respective slices of fame.

Roy Wood   Rick Price

Other memorable shows followed at the Guildhall, enabling me to smuggle a camera in, push my way to the front to watch and record a few segments of Jethro Tull and The Who. This is a favourite photo of Ian Anderson in a classic pose as Martin Barre took a solo break. Again, avoiding using a flash gun which would have drawn attention to me, followed by a swift ejection out into the street.

Jethro Tull
Ian Anderson – Martin Barre

The Tull photo was captured by using a fast 400 ASA HP black and white film, needed for low light work but resulting in a 'grainy' effect, although enhancing the print.

I also used a fast Kodachrome colour film when the Who came to town, resulting in a few blurred images as shown in the next image

Pete Townsend in mid-flight at the Guildhall

Keith Moon

Drummer Keith Moon's crazy technique was far too hectic to take a clear picture, but does give a flavour of his incredible style. He actually inspired Jim Henson of the Muppet Show, leading to 'Animal' the show's percussionist as can be clearly seen by those who have seen Moonie in action. They also appeared at the Top Rank Suite a couple of years before this show, which saw me using my contacts to go backstage, just as they appeared out of their dressing room leading to the rear of the revolving stage. As a big fan, I tried to talk to them, but their glazed eyes with fixed indicated the use of pills or something else as they walked straight past everyone in readiness to blast the dance hall out. Once again the show was good and loud, as I had managed to leave the backstage area straight to the front barrier, just a few feet away from Pete Townsend.

He changed guitar every few numbers, with busy roadies trying to keep up with his demonic playing – always seemed an angry young man. He seemed upset when the next guitar went out of tune, which was quickly taken off and thrown down onto the floor, probably causing some damage. There was a bit of a break in between songs as Pete picked up his next instrument, when he overheard the guy next to me (a fellow musician) who was moaning about the wanton destructive use of expensive guitars. Townsend glared straight at him saying *"Well – it's my f*****g money ain't it?"*.

THE END IN SIGHT

Although I was still enjoying the music and the photography as the new decade swept in, I felt that I was treading water in many ways. None of my Sixties bands had a brush with fame, apart from supporting a few chart names but much of it due to never really getting stuck into our own song-writing. We had all been 'cover' bands, lacking the incentive to knuckle down to serious composing, with the exception of Eddie Harnett whose prolific output with Heaven and later bands over in the USA gained a lot of respect.

Towards the end of the Woolston run, we had prophetically changed our name to The End. Guitarist Roy Perry had been writing stuff for a few years, but never had the chance to have anything recorded, until a stroke of good fortune cropped up. Drummer Tony Burnett was an old pal of the UK's top record producers, whose biggest success came by overseeing ground-breaking albums by the Moody Blues. 'Days Of Future Passed' released in 1967 had elevated them to global status. Tony Clarke had kept in touch with our own Tony, who cheekily asked if our little outfit could be auditioned? This was quickly arranged, seeing us travelling up to London to record a few of Roy's songs at Regent Sound Studios at no.4 Denmark Street, known as 'Tin Pan Alley'.

We were very excited at simply standing on the same spots where the Rolling Stones and many more famous names had started out just a few years before our attempt to break it big! Sadly, fame and fortune eluded us, soon becoming apparent that we were not what Tony Clarke was looking for as we all listened to the playbacks. Despite this, it was simply a great experience for us all to have at least had a go at it, before driving back home to reality.

Regent Sound Studio Soho

Photo courtesy Michael Lazarev

These final images of The End were taken at the wedding of Tony and Wendy Burnett in 1970, as I had been asked to be the official photographer for the couple. Following the church ceremony, we all piled back to the reception hotel, enjoying a superb meal, drinks, dressed in suits as befitted the occasion. We had always worn smart casual clothes for our stage shows, so these are rare images indeed, but nice memories of more great buddies who have kept in touch ever since, apart from losing Roy Perry. His father Bill was a well known businessman in the area, owning the classy Celebrity Club in Hamble by the river as well as other clubs and interests.

David   Roy

Tony   Graham

1990 gave me the chance to organise a re-union gig with this last band of my group years, linking in with another hook-up of the Itchen Grammar School thirty year anniversary from the 1960 intake. For some reason we were not able to get back to the old stamping ground, so arranged a Sunday afternoon at the nearby Obelisk pub. A glorious summer day as we set up in the beer garden with a full house enjoying the sun, barbecue and music. My camera and camcorder were on hand, so letting my friends borrow them to grab a few photos and video clips. The edited footage can be found on my YouTube channel by a simple search, which shows drummer Ronnie Allen filling in for Tony Burnett, who had moved to Eastbourne some time before

Graham David Ronnie Roy

My own driving experiences saw me change my beloved, but worn out rusty Consul for a classic 1960 Jaguar 3.4 manual with overdrive, in British Racing Green colour plus a sun roof as an added luxury in the absence of air-conditioning in most vehicles on the road.

A much-missed Jag, parked outside my old Ludlow Infants School 1970

It set me back £125 (£1682) being a lot of money to me at that time due to a very low income, but with generous parents who helped me out with an interest-free loan. It was a joy to drive with the wonderful smell of leather seats, but far too extravagant as I had not really allowed for the expensive parts and services needed by specialist garages. Within a short time, my euphoria turned to concerns as the gearbox started to cause problems, with a stick shift that would not allow me to change gears smoothly. It was not a simple case of topping up the oil, so she had to go! Not sure how much I sold it for, but not losing too much on the deal, then back to yet another cheap Ford model!

I shudder to think what this car would be worth if still around today, some estimates showing between £20-30,000, depending on condition. The same thoughts have gone through many of my musician pals who sold off their vintage Fender and Gibson guitars when first starting out in the business as they 'settled down' into marriage etc! Benefit of hindsight is a rare commodity in life.

'Z- Cars' was a popular television series during the early Sixties, set in the mythical suburb of 'Newtown' in the North West of England. The title loosely referred to the police cars, used to chase villains in this hard-hitting portrayal of the force illustrating the grim reality of the new wave of 'reality' type broadcasting. Marion Feltham's father had another perfect used car on his lot, so £70 was handed over in return for my own Z Car. This model was in the same white colour, with red leather interior, a beautiful car than was a joy to own.

A much-missed Zephyr

Just before being united with this latest car, I had needed temporary wheels after offloading the Jaguar, so splashed out on another old banger- a yellow Vauxhall Cresta, registration YOW 15, a number plate that would be much sought after in these inflationary times. My

Zephyr would soon take me away from Southampton, when finally deciding to make a giant leap forward into the great unknown in the summer of 1972. One of my other friends was Tony Pancaldi who had just changed his name to Tony Ravel, to suit his smooth 'Rat Pack' style of singing. We both knew that Southampton was not the place to further our careers, deciding to make the big break by moving up to London, believing streets were paved with gold! Early 1972 saw me purchase my first decent instrument, an EKO 12 string electric guitar as I had always loved the full sound that boosted many hits before. The Byrds had influenced me, with their electric folk/rock output that accompanied the new 'hippy' culture, along with other top name guitarists who used it to good effect.

I buckled down to refresh my basic talent, with the aid of a chord book, working out the keys and arrangements needed to compile a solo set list. Using a combination of my old songs across the years, complemented by the latest chart hits, I was soon ready to launch myself head forward into this next all-important phase of my career. It was an exciting time, not knowing where the future would take me, but unhindered by any worries or fears as befits a 23 year old. The big day came as we packed our bags into my trusty Ford, ready to hit the road up to the capital and whatever lay beyond. The next part of my show-biz Odyssey will feature in a later book, with Southern Roots – Part Two following on from this one.

"Regrets – I've had a few, but then again- too few to mention.."

Sounds familiar? We all look back to think what we might have done differently as a youngster, but life is full of twists and turns. One never knows what will happen at any given time with the future ahead of us. I would have liked to played better guitar but happy with what I know as it served its purpose during my later solo entertainment years. My writing interest, with a love of words might have led to some degree of song-writing, with just one hit record that might have boosted my career? If I had kept up with my piano side, it could have enhanced this creative side? Many a 'one hit wonder' enjoyed longevity success over many years, leading to other avenues in show-business. My unusual spin-off as a prolific TV quiz show contestant since 1982 has served as another taste of mini-celebrity status, with over thirty appearances on television screens, leading to a Guinness World Record as previously mentioned.

These formative years gave me a good grounding as a 'jack of all trades', gradually morphing into what lay ahead. I count my blessings, having been lucky in life, not really wishing to change a thing. The summer problems of 2020 forced me into an unexpected 'retirement' due to the closure of entertainment venues across the UK, but this is a temporary hiccup as far as I am concerned. It has given me time to write this book, with more on the way soon, so this cloud does have a silver lining. Losing a few more friends from my group years is a natural downside to getting old, but I am more than happy to share some of their memories in book form or across my own web-pages.

I hope you have enjoyed these personal ramblings into the sights and sounds of a different era, which may have brought nostalgic memories if you were part of it all. Younger musicians and fans of the culture will have hopefully got a taste of what their parents got up to back in their own youth. I very much doubt if I will see the invention of a time machine during my last few years, but you can guess where I would be setting the controls for...

David St John

Printed in Great Britain
by Amazon